MW01505400

THE JOURNAL FOR US

10 CONVERSATIONS
EVERY COUPLE NEEDS TO HAVE

REBEKAH LYONS
& GABE LYONS

ZONDERVAN
BOOKS

ZONDERVAN BOOKS

The Journal for Us
Copyright © 2025 by Rebekah Lyons and Gabe Lyons

Published in Grand Rapids, Michigan, by Zondervan. Zondervan is a registered trademark of The Zondervan Corporation, L.L.C., a wholly owned subsidiary of HarperCollins Christian Publishing, Inc.

Requests for information should be addressed to customercare@harpercollins.com.

Zondervan titles may be purchased in bulk for educational, business, fundraising, or sales promotional use. For information, please email SpecialMarkets@Zondervan .com.

ISBN 978-0-310-36550-1 (hardcover)

Unless otherwise noted, Scripture quotations are taken from The Holy Bible, New International Version®, NIV®. Copyright © 1973, 1978, 1984, 2011 by Biblica, Inc.® Used by permission of Zondervan. All rights reserved worldwide. www.Zondervan .com. The "NIV" and "New International Version" are trademarks registered in the United States Patent and Trademark Office by Biblica, Inc.®

Scripture quotations marked ESV are taken from the ESV® Bible (The Holy Bible, English Standard Version®). Copyright © 2001 by Crossway, a publishing ministry of Good News Publishers. Used by permission. All rights reserved.

Any internet addresses (websites, blogs, etc.) and telephone numbers in this book are offered as a resource. They are not intended in any way to be or imply an endorsement by Zondervan, nor does Zondervan vouch for the content of these sites and numbers for the life of this book.

All rights reserved. No part of this publication may be reproduced, stored in a retrieval system, or transmitted in any form or by any means—electronic, mechanical, photocopy, recording, or any other—except for brief quotations in printed reviews, without the prior permission of the publisher.

This book is intended for informational and educational purposes only and does not constitute professional advice. Readers should consult licensed professionals, such as therapists or counselors, for personalized guidance and support. The author and publisher disclaim any liability for actions taken based on the information provided in this book.

Authors are represented by Meredith Brock at The Brock Agency.

Cover design: Lindy Kasler
Cover illustration: Shutterstock
Interior design: Kait Lamphere

Printed in India

25 26 27 28 29 30 31 32 33 /RPI/ 13 12 11 10 9 8 7 6 5 4 3 2 1

WELCOME LETTER FROM GABE AND REBEKAH

We're so glad you decided to invest in your marriage by picking up this journal!

Like yours, our marriage has had its fair share of ups and downs. And years of honest conversations with wise mentors have helped us navigate the most difficult terrain together. In this journal, we're passing along many of the key lessons we've learned along the way.

Specifically, we've curated a list of ten conversations every couple needs to have. The prompts will help you address hidden tension, see each other's perspective, and get on the same page. The unity you'll enjoy on the other side of these talks can transform your marriage.

We had no idea what was possible when we began to intentionally merge our rhythms and commit to be on mission together. Life has never felt fuller and more flourishing, and every day brings new encounters that keep our energy high and faith flourishing.

We've truly begun to experience the power of us, and we want you to know what it feels like. We want you to thrive—not just survive—in your marriage.

And it all starts with a simple conversation.

Let's begin!

Gabe and Rebekah

Honest conversations are the foundation
of a thriving marriage.

GABE AND REBEKAH

CONTENTS

HOW TO USE THIS JOURNAL

The book you hold in your hands offers a unique experience. With a mix of discussion prompts and journaling exercises, *The Journal for Us* invites you to explore your thoughts alone and prepares you to share as a couple.

As we guide you through the ten conversations, you'll see different prompts along the way. Here's what to look for:

Reflect. The journal prompts will help you and your spouse prepare your thoughts for each conversation. Allow yourself twenty minutes and find a quiet space to respond in the section provided. You can each write in the space provided, but we encourage you to purchase two journals so you can write separately and share the reflections later.

Talk. After you've prepared your thoughts, the prompts will help you start the conversation. Each topic may require multiple discussions. Don't rush this. The goal is to process your thoughts and feelings with each other, no matter how long it takes.

Discover. During and following each conversation, space is provided to note what you learn about each other's perspectives. Take time alone to pray about and discern any ideas for changes you'd like to make to your marriage in the areas you're discussing. Then come together to decide how to move forward in unity.

While each "Reflect" and "Discover" section is designed to take about twenty minutes, we encourage you to set aside more time for your conversations. Take this journal on a date night or a getaway or talk while the kids are napping. Give each other time to process through these important subjects. We know how demanding life can be. Even so, don't allow your schedule to stand between you and a thriving marriage.

Throughout the journal, you'll see "Conversation Skills Check-ins." We don't just cover the *what* of conversations; we also explain the *how*. We teach several communication skills on pages 11–20 and then remind you to put them into practice throughout the journal.

HOW TO HAVE HEALTHY CONVERSATIONS

WHY CONVERSATIONS MATTER

In the fight for our marriage, we often get stuck in our head. We run through scenarios and replay responses. We have assumptions about each other that often don't match reality. It's easy to get caught in a loop about everything that's wrong, with no way back to what can be right.

When couples are committed to a healthy marriage, they stop assuming and start talking. Bringing our inner thoughts and fears into the light strips them of their power and allows us to make meaningful progress *toward* each other. These conversations can be difficult at first, but they'll get easier as you have more of them. The deep work of repair is difficult, but the results are worth it.

When couples are committed to a healthy marriage, they stop assuming and start talking.

Marriage is a lifelong adventure of discovery. We're never done getting to know our spouse, because life has a way of changing us. As the years roll on, all of us slowly evolve. We deal with heartache differently. We hit goals and make new ones. Throughout the journey, conversation is the tether that can keep you close to each other.

Whether we've been together five months or five decades, the fight for each other never stops. The battle is too epic, the outcome too important, to sit back and assume we have this figured out. Instead, we must do everything we can, in God's strength and with his guidance, to pursue a marriage that thrives, even in the face of adversity.

Your marriage is worth fighting for. Every last bit.

LEARNING HOW TO TALK AGAIN

Our youngest daughter, Joy, is adopted. Soon after bringing her home from China at age five and a half, she developed an adorable babble we called "Chinglish," mixing words from Chinese and English. As she slowly grew more comfortable with her second language, she started to mimic us. She would even hold her hand to her head, pretending it was an iPhone, jibber-jabbering away.

Early on, her absolute favorite word was *broccoli* (thankfully she liked to eat it too). But when Joy said *broccoli*, it came out *block-lee*. Even though the word didn't sound quite right, Joy was very proud of herself for knowing this word. We have dozens of videos of her declaring *block-lee* over and over.

Just like Joy, each one of us had to learn how to talk. We did this by listening, observing, repeating words, and practicing them over and over. After years of effort, we figured out how to string sentences together, how to control our tone of voice and volume, and, ultimately, how to connect with people through conversation.

As adults, we never outgrow the need to "learn how to talk." The skills we need to master as we age become more nuanced and complex. Exchanging information may equal communication, but it doesn't always result in connection. And deep, intimate, emotional connection is what all of us desperately crave.

The problem is that cultivating emotional intimacy in marriage is tough. If we're being honest, marriage can get old. Without even trying, we fall into the same old routines, have the same old fights, and ask the same old questions:

"How was your day?"

"Fine, how was yours?"

Between the overwhelm of work and parenting and life responsibilities, it doesn't take much for us to miss each other. The very person you promised to love and cherish feels at times like a stranger living in your home. You discover that you have no clue anymore what the other person truly wants and needs.

Exchanging information may equal communication, but it doesn't always result in connection.

I (Rebekah) learned this lesson through Joy. It was the summer of 2023, and our family was enjoying, as a graduation gift for our kids, all that Italy had to offer. Whenever we'd sit down for a meal at a local restaurant, Joy would ask for *block-lee*. I would order it for her, but when it arrived, she would push it away.

After a few of these incidents, I noticed Joy's tiny hand pointing to my water on the table. I asked her to repeat what she wanted, and it clicked. She wasn't saying *block-lee*; she was saying *splahk-ling*! She had discovered sparkling water, and her inner diva couldn't get enough. No tap water for this princess—she wanted Pellegrino!

I heard something close to *broccoli* and assumed I knew what Joy wanted. This is a perfect picture of how we treat our spouses. In the rush of life, it's easy to jump to conclusions. We fail to slow down and be curious. We operate on past experiences, wrong assumptions, and our own personality preferences. Very few of us do this on purpose. The truth is that most couples want to go deep with each other, but we lose sight of each other over time or we simply don't know how.

That's why Gabe and I created this conversation journal. We believe connection is the key to unlocking emotional intimacy. This book is our invitation to "learn how to talk," no matter how old you are. The right conversation will help you stop fighting *with* each other and start fighting *for* each other.

If you commit to practicing these skills and giving vulnerability a chance, your marriage will reach heights you never thought possible. You will experience the most profound connection possible—being fully known and fully loved.

The right conversation will help you stop fighting with *each other and start fighting* for *each other.*

HEALTHY CONVERSATION SKILLS

This journal contains ten important conversations every couple needs to have. But we don't just provide the topics you need to discuss; we teach you *how* to discuss them with five tried-and-true techniques.

Like any other life skill, conversation requires practice. Many of us were never taught these techniques or saw them modeled in a healthy way. But don't despair. It's never too late to learn. Think of these five skills as tools in your tool belt. As you work through this journal, you'll have plenty of opportunities to pull out these tools and put them to use.

SKILL #1: Active Listening

Having great conversations starts not with talking but with listening.

Active listening is a term that encompasses a couple other skills we'll unpack. Through active listening, you're 100 percent focused on what your spouse is telling you. You put away your phone and minimize all other distractions. You show interest by making eye contact and leaning in.

Bottom line—active listening is generously giving your spouse the gift of undivided attention.

Active listening is generously giving your spouse the gift of undivided attention.

In his book *Life Together*, Dietrich Bonhoeffer contends that listening is an act of love. First, he describes what it's like when we *don't* practice active listening:

> So often Christians, especially preachers, think that their only service is always to have to "offer" something when they are together with other people. They forget that listening can be a greater service. . . .
>
> There is also a kind of listening with half an ear that presumes already to know what the other person has to say. This impatient, inattentive listening really despises the other Christian and finally is only waiting to get a chance to speak and thus to get rid of the other.[1]

Ouch. Been there, done that. Countless times in our marriage, we've listened to each other with "half an ear," waiting for our turn to speak and offering unwelcome solutions. By contrast, Bonhoeffer says, "We do God's work for our brothers and sisters when we learn to listen to them."[2]

Notice that he used the word *learn*. Active listening is a lifelong skill.

To make this practical, here is a checklist you can reference to know what active listening looks like:

- ☐ Put away your phone (and eliminate all other distractions).
- ☐ Position your body to face your spouse.

- ☐ Look your spouse in the eye.
- ☐ Nod to show you understand.
- ☐ Ask follow-up questions to figure out what is being left unsaid.
- ☐ Withhold judgment and advice.

I (Gabe) want to add a quick note about eye contact and facing each other. In our work with couples—and speaking from personal experience—I've seen many husbands at their most comfortable in opening up to their spouses by standing shoulder to shoulder instead of eye to eye.

Men, if being vulnerable is difficult, try having a conversation while doing something active with your wife. Whether it's going for a walk, cooking, playing golf, or gardening, processing hard things often gets easier when we're engaged in movement.

SKILL #2: Mirroring

Mirroring is exactly what it sounds like—acting as a reflection for someone else. When we mirror, we project back to our spouse what we're seeing, hearing, and feeling. Mirroring helps our spouse feel deeply connected and understood.

Imagine that your spouse comes home from a stressful day and wants to vent. They're talking quickly, their eyebrows are scrunched, and they're frowning. How weird would it feel to look up at you and see you with bright eyes and a big smile on your face. At best, they'd feel misunderstood; at worst, they'd feel mocked.

Mirroring helps our spouse feel deeply connected and understood.

Proverbs 25:20 describes this experience perfectly: "Like one who takes away a garment on a cold day, or like vinegar poured on a wound, is one who sings songs to a heavy heart."

Thankfully, mirroring helps us avoid this mistake. And we practice mirroring through two primary means: our body language and our words.

With *words*, we can repeat back what we're hearing from our spouse, saying things like:

What I hear you saying is _____.
It seems like you're feeling _____.
       Is that correct?

With *body language*, be very careful about what your face, arms, and hands are expressing as you listen to your spouse. Are your arms crossed, communicating defensiveness? Are your eyes wandering, communicating boredom?

You can even go so far as to subtly mimic your spouse's facial expressions so they can see their own experience playing out in you. Don't overdo it, but the point of mirroring is to match the emotional energy you are receiving from your spouse.

SKILL #3: Being Empathetic

When Gabe and I started marriage counseling, one of the first things our therapist told us was, "You guys don't know how to practice empathy for each other."

He was right. We were defensive, each of us concerned with expressing *my side of the story*. We were truly unable to hear where the other person was coming from—which is the heart of **empathy**. Empathy expert Elizabeth Segal puts it this way:

"Empathy is about feeling and understanding the experiences of others,"[3] which Gabe and I had to learn how to do.

Being empathetic looks like honoring and listening to *their side of the story*. It looks like identifying what your spouse is feeling and letting them know you see it. When you put yourself in your spouse's shoes, you gain new insights and rewrite your own story in light of the information your spouse is bringing to the table. This shared vulnerability will forge a deep connection between the two of you.

On top of the good it does for your marriage, empathy is also good for your mental health. In *Building a Resilient Life*, I wrote, "Psychological research has shown that both giving and receiving empathy promote psychological health and help us forge connection, reduce stress, and prevent burnout."[4]

When you're practicing empathy, your goal is not to fix each other; it's to understand each other. And this shared understanding can lay the foundation for emotional intimacy.

> *When you're practicing empathy, your goal is not to fix each other; it's to understand each other. And this shared understanding can lay the foundation for emotional intimacy.*

SKILL #4: Disarming

Tension. You know it when you feel it, right? It starts to build in the air, maybe even in your body, and one wrong look or word can be the spark that ignites a bomb. Over time, as tension escalates and explodes and starts all over again, we get caught in a "crazy cycle" of conflict.

I (Rebekah) wrote in my book *Rhythms of Renewal* about how, in these cycles, "fights increase, hurt cuts deep, and spouses emotionally pull away. Once this kind of toxic cycle is in place, it can be hard to correct, and with that cycle comes increased stress, anxiety, and pain."[5]

Years ago, Gabe and I were stuck in one of these cycles and sought counsel from a wise author and marriage expert. After listening to us bicker, he gave us a wonderful tool to break out of our dysfunctional dance—the disarming technique.

Disarming is an intentional choice to deescalate someone who is complaining or blaming. We primarily disarm through our word choice. Our counselor noticed that Gabe and I were using words like, "You always," "You never," and "This is who you are." He called this "character assassination" because our extreme language painted an inaccurate picture of the other person. This accusatory language usually leads to stonewalling and defensiveness.

Disarming is an intentional choice to deescalate someone who is complaining or blaming.

Using "I" statements instead of "you" statements is one technique for disarming your spouse. For example, instead of saying, "You always do this, and you'll never change," which isn't constructive, you could say something like, "When this happened, I felt hurt." You're still addressing the issue, but you're framing it around your own experience.

Another disarming technique is to offer a caveat when expressing something negative. If your spouse has done something hurtful and you're going to bring it up, try saying something like, "I'm not saying this was your intent, but when you said or did [insert action or words], I felt [negative emotion]."

By giving your spouse the benefit of the doubt and acknowledging the truth in their experience, you minimize the possibility of escalating the tension or causing them to shut down.

SKILL #5: Telling the Truth

Pause and consider these questions: What are you withholding from your spouse? What secrets are you keeping? What grief or fears are you struggling with in silence?

Sadly, many of us find ourselves in lonely marriages, hiding shameful or fear-filled parts of ourselves from the person who is supposed to know us better than anyone else. As much as we try to cope and cover up, deep down we crave honesty.

Author and theologian Frederick Buechner wrote:

> What we hunger for perhaps more than anything else is to be known in our full humanness, and yet that is often just what we also fear more than anything else. It is important to tell at least from time to time the secret of who we truly and fully are—even if we tell it only to ourselves—because otherwise we run the risk of losing track of who we truly and fully are and little by little come to accept instead the highly edited version which we put forth in hope that the world will find it more acceptable than the real thing.[6]

Telling the truth is essential to remaining in touch with who we are. It's the foundation of intimacy. We cannot be fully loved if we are not fully known.

And we believe that telling the truth is done best through the lens of confession, allowing us to have the freedom and safety to admit what's really going on inside. Whether we're feeling hurt, angry, sad, betrayed, or lonely, confession brings these painful experiences to the light, where we can begin to examine and make sense

Telling the truth is essential to remaining in touch with who we are. It's the foundation of intimacy. We cannot be fully loved if we are not fully known.

of them. And what a beautiful gift it is to do so in the presence of our trusted spouse.

When we keep secrets, our outsides don't match our insides. Jesus spoke about this issue in Matthew 23, where he told the Pharisees that while the outside of the cup may be clean, if the inside is dirty, the cup is dirty. A mind and body that are in disunity cannot function well. This situation switches us into survival mode—fight, flight, or freeze—because we're dealing with an internal conflict.

Telling the truth paves the way for healing, for you individually and for the two of you together. As you heal, you will learn to bring your inner truth into alignment with your outer actions. And you will find that you can bring your whole, authentic self to your spouse, without fear of shame and blame.

Here are a few practical principles for confession:

- Before confessing to another person, first confess to God (Psalm 51:4; 1 John 1:9).
- Commit to radical honesty with God, yourself, and others (Psalm 32:5; Proverbs 28:13; James 5:16).
- Practice vulnerability by asking for help (Galatians 6:2).

CONVERSATION SKILLS CHECKLIST

Throughout the pages that follow, we'll guide you into practicing these skills. Here's a list of takeaways, with useful phrases to make application easy. Refer to these pages before your next conversation to keep these skills top of mind.

Active Listening

Ask yourself:

- Am I giving my spouse my undivided attention?
- Am I practicing curiosity and asking follow-up questions?

Say this:

- Tell me more about _____.

Mirroring

Ask yourself:

- Are my body language and facial expressions reflecting my spouse's emotions?

Say this:

- What I hear you saying is . . .
- It seems like you're feeling _____. Is that correct?

Being Empathetic

Ask yourself:

- Can I give my spouse the floor and let them share their side of the story?
- Am I trying to fix my spouse or am I trying to understand them?

Say this:

- Thank you for sharing. I am with you and for you.

Disarming

Ask yourself:
- Am I character assassinating my spouse by blaming them?
- Am I giving my spouse the benefit of the doubt?

Say this (use "I" statements to frame your experience instead of "you" statements):
- I'm not saying this was your intention, but when you did/said _____, I felt _____.

Telling the Truth

Ask yourself:
- What secrets am I keeping from my spouse?
- What areas of my life need to be brought into the light?

Say this:
- There's something I need to confess, and I feel _____ to say it.
- Will you pray with/for me about this issue?

THE TEN
CONVERSATIONS

WHAT WE LONG FOR

We all are born into the world looking

for someone looking for us.

CURT THOMPSON, PHD

# REFLECT

Falling in Love

> Now faith is confidence in what we hope for and assurance about what we do not see. (Hebrews 11:1)

Think back to the early days of your relationship when you were falling in love. Back then, dreams came easily. Hopes were high. You looked forward to a bright future, confident that the overwhelming love you felt for each other would carry you through anything.

Fast-forward through your perfect wedding, the honeymoon, a few kids or mortgages later, and you're confronted with the harsh reality that "happily ever after" takes some work.

How would you describe the deeper longing you had for your relationship when you were first married? What did you hope it would look like to be seen, known, and loved?

....
....
....
....
....
....
....
....

Conversation Skills Check-in

Remember, the goal of **empathy** is to understand your spouse, not to fix them.

Choosing Each Other

Love is patient and kind; love does not envy or boast; it is not arrogant or rude. It does not insist on its own way; it is not irritable or resentful; it does not rejoice at wrongdoing, but rejoices with the truth. Love bears all things, believes all things, hopes all things, endures all things. (1 Corinthians 13:4–7 ESV)

As we've learned—and as research confirms—the "in love" feeling lasts about two years. After that, love is a choice, a covenant, a commitment.[7]

If it's true that the "in love" feeling doesn't last and love then becomes a choice, covenant, and commitment, when would you say that the transition happened for you? How did you and your relationship change as a result?

....
....
....
....
....
....
....
....
....
....
....

Conversation Skills Check-in

Practice **mirroring** by reflecting your spouse's emotions through your body language and expressions.

"As Good as It Gets"

> May the God of hope fill you with all joy and peace as you trust
> in him, so that you may overflow with hope by the power of the
> Holy Spirit. (Romans 15:13)

You can begin marriage with the best of intentions, seeking intimacy and safety, but over time, with failures and traumas, you may find yourself missing the mark. Discouraged and exhausted, you hear a defeated whisper: *Maybe this is as good as it gets*. Resignation settles in, and you lose all hope for the intimate, passionate marriage you once longed for.

Resignation means deliberately giving up. It's the pathway to despair, stealing belief that healing is possible and leaving you in a fog of disconnection.

Resignation says, "It is what it is." Despair says, "I don't think I can do this." In what ways, if any, have you been tempted by or given in to resignation and despair in your marriage? What has it caused you to long for in its place?

....

....

....

....

....

....

....

Conversation Skills Check-in

Practice **active listening** by giving your spouse your full, undivided attention during conversations.

TALK

You've spent some time reflecting on longing in your marriage. Now let's talk about it.

Fully Known and Fully Loved

The heart's longing centers around the desire to be fully known and fully loved. This level of intimacy requires radical vulnerability—letting each other in.

Ask each other:

What scares you about telling the truth?

....
....
....
....
....
....
....
....
....
....
....
....

As scary as it is, being fully known requires us to live in the light, to tell the truth quickly and often. While doing so may seem daunting, Paul David Tripp reminds us, "Confession is all about hope."[8] In other words, it is the antidote to resignation and despair.

Ask each other:

What makes you hopeful about telling the truth?

....
....
....
....
....
....
....
....

Conversation Skills Check-in

In this conversation, I will practice:

- ☐ active listening
- ☐ mirroring
- ☐ being empathetic
- ☐ disarming
- ☐ telling the truth

One practical way to tell the truth is to assess where you are right now. Use these four questions to take inventory:

What's Right?

What is going well in our marriage? Where are we strong?

....
....
....
....
....
....
....

What's Wrong?

Where are we struggling in our marriage? What is painful?

....
....
....
....
....
....
....
....

What's Confused?

Where is there misunderstanding or lack of clarity?

....
....
....
....
....
....
....
....

What's Missing?

What is not currently a part of our life that we want to include?

....
....
....
....
....
....
....

DISCOVER

Fighting to Be Known

You were once darkness, but now you are light in the Lord. Live as children of light (for the fruit of the light consists in all goodness, righteousness, and truth) and find out what pleases the Lord. Have nothing to do with the fruitless deeds of darkness, but rather expose them. It is shameful even to mention what the disobedient do in secret. But everything exposed by the light becomes visible—and everything that is illuminated becomes a light. This is why it is said: "Wake up, sleeper, rise up from the dead, and Christ will shine on you." (Ephesians 5:8–14)

Take time to reflect on your conversation in the writing spaces below. If you'd like to, you can use the skill of **active listening** to take notes about what your spouse says while you talk.

During your conversation, what did you learn about yourself?

....
....
....
....
....
....
....
....
....
....
....
....
....

What did you learn about your spouse?

....
....
....
....
....
....
....
....
....

It's likely that this conversation shined a light on incongruities in your relationship. Discovering this reality can drive you in two directions: giving up or fighting. And friend, your marriage is worth fighting for.

Instead of isolating yourself and settling for incongruities, cry out to God in your desperation. He has the power to heal what is broken and restore what has been taken. When we choose to be honest with God, it paves the way to be honest with each other.

Journal a prayer below, asking God to intervene and shine his light on your marriage.

....
....
....
....
....
....
....
....
....

TALK

After reflecting on your first conversation, make time for a second one to follow up and discover even more.

Choose Hope

Your deeper longing has a purpose, which is to lead you into a more intimate and honest relationship in your marriage. Refuse to live in resignation and despair. Instead, move toward the hope found in confession.

Now it's time to practice the act of confession. Ask each other:

In this season of our marriage, what do you long for? What life do you dream of?

....
....
....
....
....
....
....
....

What can we do to start creating the life we want together?

....
....
....
....
....
....
....

> ### Conversation Skills Check-in
>
> In this conversation, I will practice:
> - ☐ active listening
> - ☐ mirroring
> - ☐ being empathetic
> - ☐ disarming
> - ☐ telling the truth

DISCOVER

As you reflect on your conversation, pray about and discern any ideas for changes you'd like to make in your marriage. After journaling on your own, schedule another time to share with your spouse what you wrote.

Dare to Dream

After learning about your deeper longings in marriage, what needs to change in your marriage? Think about your commitments, the way you talk to each other, your work responsibilities, and so forth.

....
....
....
....
....
....
....
....
....
....

What is one thing you can do this week to meet each other's deeper longings?

. . . .

. . . .

. . . .

. . . .

. . . .

. . . .

. . . .

. . . .

. . . .

. . . .

HOW WE FIGHT

*No one can dance with a partner and not touch
each other's raw spots. We must know what these
raw spots are and be able to speak about them
in a way that pulls our partner closer to us.*

DR. SUE JOHNSON, *HOLD ME TIGHT*

REFLECT

The Dysfunctional Dance

Every couple has a dance. And no, we're not talking about moving to music; we're talking about the way we relate to each other.

Like a well-rehearsed foxtrot, when momentum is good and the pathways are clear, we stay in step with each other—smooth and consistent around the dance floor. But when a sour note interrupts our rhythm, we step on each other's toes and eventually land on our rears. These patterned ways of relating become a sort of "dysfunctional dance" we step into that illuminates *how we fight* when we feel tense, distant, anxious, or alone.

You know you've begun your dysfunctional dance when something your partner says or does triggers a negative emotion you don't want to feel or acknowledge.

When was the last time you entered into your dysfunctional dance?

....

....

....

....

....

....

....

....

....

....

....

....

....

....

What negative emotion did you not want to feel or acknowledge?

....
....
....
....
....
....
....
....
....
....
....
....
....

> ## Conversation Skills Check-in
>
> To improve **active listening**, stay curious and ask your spouse follow-up questions to gain a fuller understanding.

Where Do We Feel Stuck?

Over time, the dysfunctional dance becomes our unspoken rules of engagement—the choreographed ways we react to unexpressed emotions. When we repeatedly hide what we feel, we develop a toxic code of conduct that creates fractured neural pathways in our brain. These pathways become patterns of behavior that are reinforced each time we practice our dance—again and again and again.

As Dr. Sue Johnson puts it, "The more you attack, the more dangerous you appear to me; the more I watch for your attack, the harder I hit back. And round and round we go."[9]

In what areas of your marriage do you feel stuck in a dysfunctional dance?

....
....
....
....
....
....
....
....
....
....
....

What is your "toxic code of conduct" when you fight? What are your go-to behaviors?

....
....
....
....
....
....
....
....
....
....

Left unchecked, this dysfunctional dance creates a seismic shift in your marriage. The initial longing for love and intimacy that once defined your relationship has been swallowed up by a new marriage identity, one fraught with fighting.

Conversation Skills Check-in

Next time you're feeling hurt, try **disarming** with this caveat: "I'm not saying this was your intention, but I felt _____ when you did _____."

The Four Conflict Patterns

In our work with couples over the years, Gabe and I have discovered that most marriages fall into one of four conflict patterns: *silent*, *intense*, *avoidant*, and *anxious*.

A **silent marriage** begins with hurt and unspoken resentment. Emotional wounds fester, leading to withdrawal and stonewalling. Though less outward conflict exists, hearts grow cold and distant. The couple's silence hides bitterness, yet beneath this pattern is a desire to deescalate conflict, sometimes reflecting restraint or a quiet pursuit of peace.

For the scales that follow, circle the number you believe most accurately describes your dynamic.

On a scale of 1–10, how well does the **silent** pattern describe your conflict style?

| 1 | 2 | 3 | 4 | 5 | 6 | 7 | 8 | 9 | 10 |

Not at all   *Yes, absolutely*

An **intense marriage** is fueled by anger and passion. Both partners are vocal, stubborn, and impulsive, enjoying the fight to win. Though it often leads to exhaustion, their energy to argue reflects deep care and commitment. They escalate quickly but reconcile just as rapidly, driven by their passion for each other—sometimes leading to makeup sex.

On a scale of 1–10, how well does the **intense** pattern describe your conflict style?

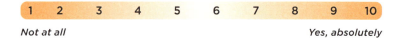

Not at all   Yes, absolutely

An **avoidant marriage** occurs when one or both partners evade conflict by shutting down or changing the subject, leading to emotional distance. While avoidance offers temporary relief, it erodes connection, leaving spouses feeling isolated. Reengaging through reflection or enlisting the help of a third party is essential to restoring communication and intimacy.

On a scale of 1–10, how well does the **avoidant** pattern describe your conflict style?

Not at all   Yes, absolutely

An **anxious marriage** is driven by fear and insecurity, with one partner constantly seeking reassurance and the other feeling burdened by the need to soothe. Anxiety can create cycles of control and frustration. However, facing these fears together builds resilience and teaches both partners to understand and manage their emotional triggers.

On a scale of 1–10, how well does the **anxious** pattern describe your conflict style?

Not at all   Yes, absolutely

TALK

You've spent some time reflecting on conflict in your marriage. Now let's talk about it.

Defining Our Dance

Share your answers to the questions on pages 39–40.

Which pattern do you identify with most as an individual? And which dance best describes your dynamic as a couple?

....
....
....
....
....
....
....
....
....
....

How did this pattern show up in your last fight?

....
....
....
....
....
....
....
....
....
....

What insights did you gain about yourself as you reflected on conflict in your marriage?

....

....

....

....

....

The secret to stopping the dance is to recognize that no one has to be the bad guy.

Dr. Sue Johnson, *Created for Connection*

....

....

....

....

....

....

DISCOVER

Take time to reflect below on your conversation. If you'd like to, you can use the skill of **active listening** to take notes about what your spouse says while you talk.

During your conversation, what did you learn about yourself?

....

....

....

....

....

....

....

....

....

What did you learn about your spouse?

....
....
....
....
....
....
....
....
....
....

Asking God for Help

Talking about fighting tends to stir up a lot of emotions and poke old wounds. And as much as we want to fix ourselves, the reality is that we need to turn to God to do the deep work of transformation.

Journal a prayer below, asking God to heal past hurts that have contributed to your conflict style. Ask him to do what only he can do to change your dysfunctional dance.

....
....
....
....
....
....
....
....
....
....

TALK

After reflecting on your first conversation, make time for a second one to follow up and go deeper.

Breaking Free from Our Dysfunctional Dance

Once you identify your primary pattern, you can begin to trace your trigger back to its source—the unresolved relational dynamic from the past that you are trying to resolve in the present.

The coping strategy that helped you survive as a child is no longer serving you well as an adult.

Growing up, you may have learned to keep your mouth shut (a silent personality style) because the ensuing conflict would otherwise lead to a tongue-lashing. Maybe you lashed out to express your anger (an intense personality style). Perhaps you withdrew to avoid hurt or hurting another's feelings (an avoidant personality style). Maybe you tried to manipulate or control others to assuage your fears (an anxious personality style).

The problem is that you've carried that unresolved pain into your marriage, and the coping strategy that helped you survive as a child is no longer serving you well as an adult.

What childhood experiences may have contributed to your conflict style?

....
....
....
....
....
....
....

What unresolved pain or relational dynamics from childhood do you recognize in your relationship?

....

....

....

....

....

....

....

....

....

....

No matter how long you've been stuck in an unhealthy conflict pattern, it's never too late to learn a new dance.

Breaking free from the dysfunctional dance begins when we allow ourselves to have compassion for the little boy or girl we once were and for what we went through. It also helps to see the little girl or boy our spouse once was.

If you could talk to that younger version of yourself, what would you say?

....

....

....

....

....

....

....

....

....

Conversation Skills Check-in

In this conversation, I will practice:

- ☐ active listening
- ☐ mirroring
- ☐ being empathetic
- ☐ disarming
- ☐ telling the truth

The next time we are locked in conflict, what do you need from me? How can I love you through it?

....
....
....
....
....
....
....
....
....
....
....
....
....
....
....
....
....
....
....
....
....

DISCOVER

As you reflect on your conversation, pray about and discern any ideas for changes you'd like to make in your marriage. After journaling on your own, schedule another time to share with your spouse what you wrote.

Fighting for Each Other, Not with Each Other

After learning about your dysfunctional dance, what needs to change in your marriage?

....
....
....
....
....
....
....

What kind of marriage are you fighting for? Describe it below:

....
....
....
....
....
....
....

Conversation Skills Check-in

To **disarm**, use "I" statements, like "I felt _____ when _____," to express your feelings.

OUR ORIGIN STORIES

Every time we get emotionally wounded, our brain stores the pain of that experience, and it becomes an area of sensitivity. If something in the present reminds us of the past hurtful experience, it becomes an emotional sore spot or area of extreme sensitivity.

DR. GREG SMALLEY

REFLECT

Looking Backward to Go Forward

If there's one thing Rebekah and I (Gabe) have learned, it's that going backward to go forward is a key growth principle in our emotional and relational health. When we better understand the significant relationships and events that shaped us in childhood, we find clues about why we act (and react) the way we do in adulthood.

My perspective for the first fifteen years of marriage with Rebekah was that going backward was a waste of time. I saw it as a diversion that kept us from moving forward in life. Out of a desire not to blame my parents or take on a victim mentality, I focused on the future. I never intentionally decided to bury my past, but it became a survival skill nonetheless. It informed how I related for years to Rebekah, my partner in my most important relationship.

How do you feel about the idea of looking backward at childhood experiences to go forward in your marriage?

....
....
....
....
....
....
....
....
....
....
....
....

What doubts, concerns, or hopes are you aware of?

....

....

....

....

....

....

....

....

....

....

> **Conversation Skills Check-in**
>
> **Tell the truth:** Don't keep secrets, even when it's uncomfortable.

Examining Childhood Experiences

Our origin stories encompass our formative experiences and family legacies. What childhood circumstances and experiences—positive and negative—stand out most to you? Take time to go back and reflect on each season of your life.

....

....

....

....

....

....

....

....

....

In what ways did these circumstances and experiences impact you as a child? For example, consider how they formed your view of yourself, your motives, and the way you related to others.

....
....
....
....
....
....
....
....
....
....
....
....

In what ways do you recognize the same childhood dynamics you just identified in your adult life and relationships?

....
....
....
....
....
....
....
....
....
....
....

The Four Attachment Styles

Attachment style is the term psychologists use to describe our default way of relating in our most important relationships.

The concept dates back to the 1950s and describes how the relationship between a caregiver and child makes or fails to make a child feel safe, secure, and protected.[10] This same attachment style then carries over into adult relationships. We typically develop one of four attachment styles: *secure, anxious, avoidant*, or *disorganized*.[11]

Secure attachment. Children with a secure attachment style often show distress when separated from and joy when reunited with their caregiver. Although upset, they feel confident the caregiver will return; and if scared, they are comfortable seeking reassurance from other caregivers. They feel the freedom to play and explore their surroundings.

Adults with a secure attachment style are largely content, secure, and able to identify and share their feelings with others. They can build and maintain stable relationships.

For the scales that follow, circle the number that best describes your attachment style.

On a scale of 1–10, how well does the secure attachment style describe you?

| 1 | 2 | 3 | 4 | 5 | 6 | 7 | 8 | 9 | 10 |

Not at all   *Yes, absolutely*

Anxious attachment. Children with an anxious attachment style have unreliable parents who may be loving and supportive one minute and unavailable or stern the next. As a result of poor parental availability, these children do not depend on their primary caregiver to be there when they need them.

Adults with an anxious attachment style lack a sense of security in themselves. They have a high emotional dependence on others and seek continued affirmation of their value and worth.[12]

On a scale of 1–10, how well does the **anxious attachment** style describe you?

Not at all   Yes, absolutely

Avoidant attachment. A child with an avoidant attachment style has caregivers who are dismissive of their feelings and often reject or disapprove of their emotional needs. As a result, the child learns to shut down their feelings and stay neutral or pleasant on the outside to protect themselves.[13]

Adults with an avoidant attachment style find emotional intimacy extremely difficult to establish, not because they don't want it, but because they don't know how to attain it.

On a scale of 1–10, how well does the **avoidant attachment** style describe you?

Not at all   Yes, absolutely

Disorganized attachment. This is the least common form of attachment, in which a child experiences trauma from caregivers through severe neglect or verbal, physical, or sexual abuse. As a result, the caregiver is a source of fear rather than security. The child tries to avoid abuse through fearful obedience, even though this approach is unreliable.[14]

Adults with a disorganized attachment style can experience distress or confusion, a lack of self-confidence, inconsistent behaviors, and an inability to trust others in intimate relationships.[15]

On a scale of 1–10, how well does the **disorganized attachment** style describe you?

| 1 | 2 | 3 | 4 | 5 | 6 | 7 | 8 | 9 | 10 |

Not at all   Yes, absolutely

In what healthy or unhealthy ways is your attachment style evident in the ways you have sought to meet your emotional and relational needs over the years? In your marriage?

....
....
....
....
....
....

TALK

You've spent some time reflecting on your origin story. Now let's talk about it.

Understanding Where You've Come From

Which attachment style (secure, anxious, avoidant, disorganized) describes you best?

....
....
....
....
....
....

Which childhood experiences shaped your attachment style?

....
....
....
....
....
....
....
....
....
....
....
....

What's something about yourself you've never told me?

....
....
....
....
....
....
....
....
....
....
....

Conversation Skills Check-in

Practicing **empathy** is worth it. By seeking to understand your spouse's perspective, you'll strengthen your emotional bond.

DISCOVER

Take time to reflect on your conversation. If you'd like to, you can use the skill of **active listening** to take notes about what your spouse says while you talk.

During your conversation, what did you learn about yourself?

....
....
....
....
....
....
....
....
....
....
....

What did you learn about your spouse?

....
....
....
....
....
....
....
....
....
....
....

God Is Writing Your Story

Psalm 139:16 reads, "All the days ordained for me were written in your book before one of them came to be."

God is the author of your story. He knows everything that has ever happened and ever will happen. Journal a prayer below, surrendering to God your role as the author of your story—where you've come from and where you're going.

....
....
....
....
....
....
....
....

TALK

After reflecting on your first conversation, make time for a second one to follow up and go deeper.

Getting to Know You

While origin stories can feel weighty, they don't always have to be. The best way to get to know your spouse often is through having fun and simply letting your curiosity guide you.

You can discover more about your spouse's childhood by simply asking questions. Feel free to ask your spouse the following questions or make up your own. Then write down their answers. This is a great opportunity to practice active listening!

Can you tell me about one place you loved to visit growing up? What made it so special?

....
....
....
....
....
....
....
....

What's a memory from your childhood that always makes you laugh?

....
....
....
....
....
....
....
....

What's one toy or hobby or game from childhood that brought you tons of joy?

....
....
....
....
....
....
....

What did you excel at?

....
....
....
....
....
....
....
....
....

What's your first memory of faith, being taught about God, or awareness of God's presence?

....
....
....
....
....
....
....
....

When you were a kid, who made you feel loved and accepted?

....
....
....
....
....
....
....
....

How is our family different from yours growing up? How is it similar?

. . . .

. . . .

. . . .

. . . .

. . . .

. . . .

. . . .

. . . .

. . . .

DISCOVER

As you reflect on your conversation, pray about and discern any ideas for changes you'd like to make in your marriage. After journaling on your own, schedule another time to share with your spouse what you wrote.

A Lifetime of Discovery

After learning about your spouse's origin story (and sharing yours), what needs to change in your marriage?

. . . .

. . . .

. . . .

. . . .

. . . .

. . . .

. . . .

. . . .

As life progresses and you both continue to grow as individuals, what are some ways you can stay connected and get to know each other, even amid life's relentless demands?

....
....
....
....
....
....
....
....
....
....

EXPRESSING OUR FEELINGS

*Emotions point us in the direction of our hurt.
They can be beacons, not barriers, helping
us identify what we most care about and
motivating us to make positive changes.*

SUSAN DAVID

REFLECT

How Easily Do You Feel Your Feelings?

For over half of our marriage, I (Gabe) had difficulty feeling my feelings. I rarely knew what emotions I was experiencing, much less giving myself permission to be curious about them. This behavior was born out of my personality, my past trauma, and my tendency to choose the dopamine of distraction over feeling unpleasant emotions.

Are you quick or slow to feel your feelings? Write about a recent experience that illustrates this tendency.

....
....
....
....
....
....
....
....

In what ways do you distract yourself or numb out when you have feelings you don't understand or that make you uncomfortable?

....
....
....
....
....
....
....
....

Conversation Skills Check-in

One way to show **empathy** is to let your spouse share their story fully without interrupting or judging.

Opposites Attract

Rebekah is the complete opposite of me. She feels deeply and easily. My inability to connect with my emotions—or the emotions of those around me—created a roadblock in our relationship. When Rebekah experienced a hard day and shared about it, I didn't truly *hear* her. Instead of connecting with her emotions, I offered up some weak solution or wooden platitude.

After years of failed attempts to meet Rebekah in her need, it became clear that for the health of our marriage, I needed to work on my emotional capacity. I'm embarrassed to say it took nearly twenty years to get to where I am today—but all the reading, therapy, confession, and slow attempts to learn are worth it.

Emotionally speaking, what does your spouse need from you that they're not receiving?

....
....
....
....
....
....
....
....
....
....
....

What do you need from your spouse that you're not receiving?

....

....

....

....

....

....

....

....

....

....

....

....

The Eight Core Emotions

One of the best tools Rebekah and I use for emotional expression is a book called *The Voice of the Heart* by Dr. Chip Dodd, in which he narrows our emotional states down to eight—*only eight?*—that help us overcome the fear of drowning in an ocean of emotions. His eight core feelings are *hurt, lonely, sad, anger, fear, shame, guilt,* and *glad.*[16]

While seven of the eight emotions may seem negative, the truth is that no emotion is negative. Each one is a gift from God, a signal that something deeper in your heart is worth paying attention to.

When you express precisely what you're feeling to your spouse, the improved understanding between you and your spouse will create a cycle of connection, taking you on an important emotional journey. By identifying any unpleasant emotions, you will also be able to identify what you lack, giving you the opportunity to have that need fulfilled.

Refer to the eight core emotions on the previous page. Which ones have you experienced recently? Write about what was happening to cause those emotions to come to the surface.

....
....
....
....
....
....
....
....
....

What unmet needs do your unpleasant emotions reveal?

....
....
....
....
....
....
....
....
....

The Power of Confession

Once again, we're going to talk about the power of confession. When we bring our emotions into the light, we move past their impairments and into the gift each emotion has to offer:

- Confessed *hurt* leads us from *resentment* to *courage*.
- Confessed *loneliness* leads us from *apathy* to *intimacy*.

- Confessed *sadness* leads us from *self-pity* to *acceptance*.
- Confessed *anger* leads us from *depression and pride* to *passion*.
- Confessed *fear* leads us from *anxiety* to *faith*.
- Confessed *shame* leads us from *contempt* to *humility*.
- Confessed *guilt* leads us from *toxic shame* to *freedom*.
- Confessed *gladness* leads us from *sensuality* to *joy*.[17]

From the list above, what do you need to confess? And what gift is waiting for you on the other side of that confession?

. . . .

. . . .

. . . .

. . . .

. . . .

. . . .

. . . .

. . . .

. . . .

. . . .

. . . .

. . . .

. . . .

. . . .

. . . .

. . . .

Conversation Skills Check-in

Confession is a way to **tell the truth**, building trust and inviting deeper intimacy.

TALK

You've spent some time reflecting on feelings. Now let's talk about them.

What Do You Need from Me?

Ask each other:

How do you distract yourself when you want to numb out from unpleasant emotions? What would happen if you chose to feel your feelings instead of running from them?

....
....
....
....
....
....
....
....
....

When it comes to emotional intimacy, what do you need from me?

....
....
....
....
....
....
....
....
....

Conversation Skills Check-in

In this conversation, I will practice:

- ☐ active listening
- ☐ mirroring
- ☐ being empathetic
- ☐ disarming
- ☐ telling the truth

 # DISCOVER

Take time to reflect below on the conversation you just had. If you'd like to, you can use the skill of **active listening** to take notes about what your spouse says while you talk.

During your conversation, what did you learn about yourself?

. . . .

. . . .

. . . .

. . . .

. . . .

. . . .

. . . .

. . . .

. . . .

. . . .

. . . .

. . . .

. . . .

. . . .

What did you learn about your spouse?

....
....
....
....
....
....
....
....

What the Bible Says About Emotions

Have you ever wondered what Scripture has to say about feeling our feelings? All you have to do is turn to the book of Psalms to find out. Most of the psalms were written by King David, who was described by God as a "man after my own heart" (Acts 13:22). The psalms are filled with his emotional cries to God. He put it all out there, from lament, mourning, and weeping to dancing, singing, and gratitude.

Turn to the book of Psalms and read a few. You could start with Psalms 13, 16, 22, and 51. As you read them, journal a prayer to God expressing any thought, emotion, hope, and fear that comes to mind. Ask God to connect with you through his Word.

....
....
....
....
....
....
....
....

TALK

After reflecting on your first conversation, make time for a second one to follow up and go deeper.

From Impairment to Gifts

Reflect on what you've learned about the eight core emotions, impairments, and gifts. Think through a specific feeling you've had recently and practice confessing it to each other.

Confess your feeling and acknowledge why you felt that way. For example, "I felt angry because it appeared you didn't value my opinion," or "I felt hurt that you didn't want sex."

....
....
....
....
....
....
....
....
....
....
....
....
....
....
....
....
....
....

Make a statement that draws on the gift of that feeling (such as courage, intimacy, acceptance, and so on) to move toward your spouse. For example, "I offered my advice because I care so much," or "I know we've been missing each other with our busy schedules."

....

....

....

....

....

....

....

....

Ask a question to help you continue moving toward each other. For example, "Is there a way I can contribute that is helpful?" or "How can we carve out some quality time together so we feel more connected?"

....

....

....

....

....

....

....

....

Conversation Skills Check-in

Tell the truth: Ask yourself, "What parts of my life do I need to bring into the light?"

DISCOVER

As you reflect on your conversation, pray about and discern any ideas for changes you'd like to make in your marriage. After journaling on your own, schedule another time with your spouse to share what you wrote and to talk through what they've written down.

The Freedom to Feel

After learning how you and your spouse express your feelings, what do you see that needs to change in your marriage?

....
....
....
....
....
....
....
....
....

Now that you've learned what your spouse needs from you, what will you do to honor that need as you move forward?

....
....
....
....
....
....
....
....

OUR FRIENDS AND COMMUNITY

God never intended couples to handle marriage and family issues alone. A community of fellow sojourners is an essential ingredient for a healthy marriage and a vibrant faith.

JIM BURNS

REFLECT

The Problem of Loneliness

Almost a decade ago, Rebekah and I were lonely. That's not to say that we were completely on our own. We had three children, two dogs, and eight million neighbors outside our lower Manhattan apartment. We were always surrounded by people, but we weren't connected to a community.

Four years earlier, we had sold most of our possessions and moved our family from the sleepy suburbs of Atlanta to the city that never sleeps. Our goal was to grow our newly founded media company, THINQ, in the very epicenter of American culture.

Several years into city life, we were having second thoughts. Life was exciting, but it was also lonely. Work was never-ending, and my schedule was packed with meetings, events, and dinners. In the chronic stress of our new life, we were beginning to realize just how few support structures we had. Our friends were just as busy as we were, and we had no family within four hundred miles. The busyness, the loneliness, the lack of structure—all of it was taking a toll on our family and marriage.

Do you relate to our story?

How would you assess the degree to which your marriage is isolated or supported in community? Circle the number on the continuum that best describes your response.

1	2	3	4	5		6	7	8	9	10

Isolation   *Community*

We have little to no connection   We have a great deal of connection
with others who support us   with others who support us

How does it feel to acknowledge this rating? What impact does your support or lack of support make in your life right now?

. . . .
. . . .
. . . .
. . . .
. . . .
. . . .
. . . .
. . . .
. . . .

Looking Back on Your Friendships

Recall the seasons you've experienced in your marriage (for example, being newlyweds; having babies, toddlers, or teens; your current season; or any season of major events, such as relocation, unemployment, medical event, and so forth).

In which season or seasons have you felt most isolated as a couple? What factors or circumstances contributed to the feeling of isolation?

. . . .
. . . .
. . . .
. . . .
. . . .
. . . .
. . . .
. . . .
. . . .

In which season or seasons have you felt most connected to community? What factors or circumstances contributed to the feeling of connectedness?

....
....
....
....
....
....
....
....
....
....
....
....

Conversation Skills Check-in

One way to practice **telling the truth** is to pray. First confess to God your need for community. Then ask your spouse to support you by praying with you and for you.

How to Build Community

So how do we find community in an age of increasing loneliness? We encourage you to look in four areas: *social structures, mentors, fellow learners,* and *friends.*

Social structures. Social structures are organizations like schools and churches that provide existing rhythms you can plug into. They provide a sense of togetherness and ease the pressure on your marriage, helping you raise children with shared values and support.

Mentors. Every marriage needs mentors—couples with a few more years of experience—who offer wisdom and guidance. They can be local or long-distance. Prioritize intentional time with them, attending retreats or virtual meetings, to ensure you're not navigating your marriage in isolation.

Fellow learners. In community, your goal should be to both receive and contribute, learning from and helping other couples. Engaging with others not only supports them but also strengthens you and your own marriage.

Friends. Friends are companions who support you through life's ups and downs. Every healthy marriage needs friends who offer hope, accountability, and a safe space where honesty is encouraged. Even a few close friends who share your values can make a powerful difference.

After reading through the four areas of community, make a list of the support you already have in each category. Notice the areas where you need more support.

....
....
....
....
....
....
....
....
....
....
....
....

TALK

You've spent some time reflecting on your friends and community. Now let's talk about them.

What Is Our Community Like?

Ask each other:

Who are your closest friends? What do you value about them?

....
....
....
....
....
....
....
....
....
....

When is the last time you felt lonely in our marriage? What circumstances contributed to it?

....
....
....
....
....
....
....
....
....

What rhythms (daily, weekly, monthly, annually) can we establish to fight loneliness in our marriage?

....

....

....

....

....

....

....

....

....

....

....

....

....

....

....

....

....

....

....

....

Conversation Skills Check-in

In this conversation, I will practice:

- ☐ active listening
- ☐ mirroring
- ☐ being empathetic
- ☐ disarming
- ☐ telling the truth

DISCOVER

Take time to reflect below on your conversation. If you'd like to, you can use the skill of **active listening** to take notes about what your spouse says while you talk.

During your conversation, what did you learn about yourself?

....
....
....
....
....
....
....
....
....
....
....

What did you learn about your spouse?

....
....
....
....
....
....
....
....
....
....
....
....

Asking God for Community

Couples grounded in community flourish, while couples in isolation run the risk of falling apart. Spend some time journaling a prayer, asking God to bless your current community and help you find new mentors and friends. What kind of connection do you find yourself longing for? Bring it to the Lord and ask him to grant you the desires of your heart.

TALK

After reflecting on your first conversation, make time for a second one to follow up and go deeper.

Making Time for Friendships

Ask each other:

Of the four categories of community (social structures, mentors, fellow learners, friends), where are we doing well? And where do we need more support?

....
....
....
....
....
....
....
....
....

Practically speaking, what do we need to change about our schedules so we can spend more time with friends?

....
....
....
....
....
....
....
....

Conversation Skills Check-in

To practice **mirroring**, clarify your spouse's emotions by asking, "It seems like you're feeling _____. Is that right?"

DISCOVER

As you reflect on your conversation, pray about and discern any ideas for changes you'd like to make in your marriage. After journaling on your own, schedule another time to share with your spouse what you wrote and to talk through what they've written down.

Making People a Priority

After discussing the state of your friends and community, what needs to change in your marriage in order to prioritize relationships?

....

....

....

....

....

....

....

....

Make a list of people you'd like to connect or reconnect with. Get out your calendar and find a few options for having them over to your house or going out for dinner. Connect with your spouse and together send an invitation to those friends.

Write your list and options below:

. . . .
. . . .
. . . .
. . . .
. . . .
. . . .
. . . .
. . . .
. . . .
. . . .

HOW WE PARTNER IN WORK

Knowing the role that God has designed your spouse to fulfill means you can support and encourage them as they grow into that role. You get to be God's voice to them as you affirm their divine calling in your marriage.

TIMOTHY AND KATHY KELLER

REFLECT

Your Unique Calling

Each human being has a divine assignment—often called a vocation—that goes beyond a nine-to-five job and transcends the limits of a job title. It's not just about what we do, but also about who we are. While not everyone may have a paid job, everyone has a calling.

Calling is where our talents and burdens collide. Our talents are our birthright gifts, the gifts that make our hearts sing, come alive. Our burdens are found in our stories, in what breaks our hearts.

Rebekah, *You Are Free*

The Latin root of the word vocation —*vocare*—means "to call." This implies there is One who calls, which means a calling begins with a caller. To be called by God is to be invited to participate in the work he is doing in the world, and this calling is based on your unique gifts, passions, and place in life.

Overall, how clear do you feel about your personal calling—the unique contribution God has called you to make in this season of life?

....
....
....
....
....
....
....
....
....
....
....

What do you need most from your spouse to help you get clarity on your calling or to begin pursuing your calling?

....

....

....

....

....

....

....

....

Conversation Skills Check-in

As your spouse talks through what their calling is and how they think they are meant to live in light of that, **disarm** them with **active listening** and ask questions to help them further unearth their calling and how you can support them in it.

Individuals Versus Partners

Our calling includes every area of life—home, church, relationships, *and* work. In addition to God's personal call on your unique life, he has placed a corporate call on your life—to be a friend and follower of Jesus and to pursue unity in the church.

What does it look like to live out God's corporate calling in marriage? Perhaps the best place to start is to look back to the beginning, when God paired Adam and Eve together in a unifying covenant—marriage—and called them to partner together. One was not subordinate to the other. Instead, they were to partner in the tasks of raising children, cultivating the earth, and glorifying God as they did so.

Gabe and I try to partner in marriage in many ways. From kid pickups and drop-offs to cooking, cleaning, and tending to the garden or chickens, our acts of cultivating the earth are shared. We also partner in leading our kids and each other into deeper relationship with God. We exercise mutual submission in taking on the daily assignments required to lead a family and live our lives together.

How would you assess the degree to which you and your spouse are operating as individuals or partners in your marriage? Circle the number on the continuum that best describes your response.

| 1 | 2 | 3 | 4 | 5 | 6 | 7 | 8 | 9 | 10 |

Individuals   *Partners*

One or both of us are unclear about our calling and do not support each other fully or equally

We both know our calling and are willing to make sacrifices to fully support each other

Reflect on your answer. Why did you choose that particular number?

....
....
....
....
....
....
....
....
....
....
....
....
....

Is Your Marriage Lopsided?

When a married couple navigates their life together and their work as individuals, there is always a danger that the relationship will become lopsided. In a lopsided marriage, the work or personal growth needs of one spouse start to dominate and have outsized influence on the couple's decision-making and the trajectory of their life as a couple and a family.

However, when a married couple navigates their life together as a partnership—where the union of two individuals creates something greater than the sum of two parts—they begin to experience what God intended. Partners in marriage are intentional about valuing the needs and opinions of each other in significant (and insignificant) matters.

While supporting each person's unique giftedness, calling, and contribution to the world, they also partner in a shared mission— one that not only brings new life to the couple but extends into their community as well.

In what ways, if any, have you experienced a lopsided dynamic in your marriage—in the distant past or more recently?

....
....
....
....
....
....
....
....
....
....

Was the lopsidedness an intentional decision you made for a season, or was it something you drifted into without really thinking about it?

....
....
....
....
....
....
....
....

If your marriage is lopsided now, what changes might you have to make to move toward a more equal partnership?

....
....
....
....
....
....
....
....

Don't Lead Parallel Lives

Researcher Dr. John Gottman warns, "Some people leave a marriage literally, by divorcing. Others do so by leading parallel lives together."[18]

Some people leave a marriage literally, by divorcing. Others do so by leading parallel lives together.

Dr. John Gottman

In order to avoid leading parallel lives, we suggest applying these three characteristics of a partnered marriage to your relationship:

Partners consider each other's gifts. They ask questions, help each other trace their origin story, and imagine possibilities beyond what their spouse might consider for themselves. Partnership requires reciprocity, which means each spouse is willing to sacrifice their own priorities to benefit their mate. Partnered couples deeply desire to cultivate each other's gifts.

Partners activate and engage by spurring each other on. When self-doubt kicks in and we ask, "Do I have what it takes?" our spouse responds with love and affirmation and calls out the ways we make an impact. In conversations with friends, our spouse brags on our latest project or venture and celebrates our wins.

Partners live a shared vision of love and good deeds. Partners ask, "What love and good deeds has God set out for us to accomplish *together*? If we could do anything together to make the world a better place, what would it be?" They contemplate how God may want to use them as a couple—even as a family—to bring healing to the world.

Of the three characteristics above, which one is strongest in your marriage? Which one needs some attention?

. . . .

. . . .

. . . .

. . . .

. . . .

. . . .

. . . .

. . . .

. . . .

. . . .

Write down a few ideas on how to practice partnership better together.

....

....

....

....

....

....

TALK

You've spent some time reflecting on how you can partner in your work. Now let's talk about it.

Getting Clear on Your Calling

If one of you is struggling with a clear sense of calling in this season, below are some of the questions Gabe asked me (Rebekah) when I needed clarity on who I was and what I had to offer.

Partner with your spouse by asking each question. Practice active listening by asking follow-up questions and saying "tell me more" about what makes you curious.

What did you dream about being one day when you were a young child?

....

....

....

....

....

....

What are your natural talents, the ones that come so easily you almost never have to exert effort?

....
....
....
....
....
....
....
....
....

What do others say you're good at?

....
....
....
....
....
....
....
....

What's wrong in the world that you wish were made right?

....
....
....
....
....
....
....
....

In this conversation, I will practice:

- ☐ active listening
- ☐ mirroring
- ☐ being empathetic
- ☐ disarming
- ☐ telling the truth

DISCOVER

Take time to reflect on your conversation. If you'd like to, you can use the skill of **active listening** to take notes about what your spouse says while you talk.

During your conversation, what did you learn about yourself?

....
....
....
....
....
....
....
....
....
....
....
....
....

What did you learn about your spouse?

....

....

....

....

....

....

....

....

....

Prepared for Good Works

Ephesians 2:10 reads, "We are God's handiwork, created in Christ Jesus to do good works, which God prepared in advance for us to do."

Reflect on how God has uniquely designed you. If you are his handiwork, what does that say about your value? And in what ways has he created you to contribute to the world?

We are God's handiwork, created in Christ Jesus to do good works, which God prepared in advance for us to do.
Ephesians 2:10

Journal a prayer below, asking God to expand your capacity and reveal the good works he has prepared for you.

....

....

....

....

....

....

....

....

TALK

After reflecting on your first conversation, make time for a second one to follow up and go deeper.

Building a Partnered Marriage

What insights do you have about your spouse's personal calling? Share with your spouse what you've observed about their unique gifts and skills. Be specific. For example, instead of saying something imprecise, such as, "You're compassionate," you might say, "You know how to make people who are hurting feel loved and safe."

....

....

....

....

....

....

....

....

....

....

....

....

....

....

....

....

In a partnered marriage, couples contemplate God's bigger vision for their marriage.

What experiences have you had in pursuing love and good works together? How did being used by God together differ from your experiences of being used by God alone?

....
....
....
....
....
....
....
....

What dreams—big or small—do you have for your shared calling? What do you hope God might be calling you to?

....
....
....
....
....
....
....
....

Conversation Skills Check-in

In this conversation, I will practice:

- ☐ active listening
- ☐ mirroring
- ☐ being empathetic
- ☐ disarming
- ☐ telling the truth

DISCOVER

As you reflect on your conversation, pray about and discern any ideas for changes you'd like to make in your marriage. After journaling on your own, schedule another time to share with your spouse what you wrote and talk through what they've written down.

Be the Partner Your Partner Needs

As we've learned, our marriages can get lopsided, favoring one person's calling over another. As you move forward as partners, be intentional to study each other, staying connected so that you're aware of each other's needs.

What support do you need from your spouse to pursue your calling? Be specific about emotional, spiritual, and practical ways they can help you.

....
....
....
....
....
....
....
....
....
....
....
....
....
....

What support does your spouse need from you? How can you provide it?

....
....
....
....
....
....
....
....
....
....
....
....

Based on what you've discovered in this conversation about partnership, what needs to change in your marriage to make room for both of your callings?

....
....
....
....
....
....
....
....
....
....
....
....

OUR PHILOSOPHY ON MONEY

God is able to bless you abundantly, so that in all things at all times, having all that you need, you will abound in every good work.

2 CORINTHIANS 9:8

REFLECT

Your Money Mindset

I (Rebekah) didn't grow up with money. My parents were teachers, which did allow me to attend the private school where they taught tuition-free.

I was among the poorest in my class from kindergarten to twelfth grade. I learned the difference between the haves and the have-nots. I compared my home-packed lunch to their fresh meals from a local deli. I compared my hand-sewn clothes to their name-brand outfits.

It's no surprise that I struggle with a scarcity mindset, given that money was always tight. Gabe, on the other hand, has what initially looks like the opposite of a scarcity mindset. He's been blessed with the gift of faith, and he believes in the power of money. Gabe assumes there will always be enough. (It's so annoying!)

Gabe's mindset is about living in the moment and embracing what brings delight now. And yet, as you'll see, there's more to Gabe's view of money than initially meets the eye, because it, too, is an expression of a scarcity mindset.

How would you assess the degree to which your marriage is characterized by either a scarcity or an abundance mindset? Circle the number on the continuum that best describes your response.

1	2	3	4	5	6	7	8	9	10

Scarcity Mindset

We make financial decisions either out of the fear that we will never have enough or in denial of our financial limits

Abundance Mindset

We make financial decisions in the faith that God will always provide and by living within our means

Reflect on your answer below. Why did you respond this way?

....

....

....

....

....

....

....

....

....

....

....

In what ways do you recognize either your scarcity or your abundance mindset in your recent purchases?

....

....

....

....

....

....

....

....

....

....

....

Money Fights

More than 41 percent of married couples strongly or somewhat agree money is a major source of fights and tension in their household.[19]

In what ways have your differing views about money sparked conflict in your marriage? Or in what ways have your shared views amplified your money problems (for example, by increasing your fears of never having enough or your denial of limits)?

....
....
....
....
....
....
....
....
....
....
....

Conversation Skills Check-in

By giving your spouse the benefit of the doubt, even when emotions run high, you **disarm** their defenses.

Cultivating an Abundance Mindset

To have a thriving marriage, it's essential to cultivate unity that leads to a shared abundance mindset. When the saver and the spender get on the same page and begin to live in Christ-centered generosity, great things can happen. The penny-pincher stops being so tightfisted. The extravagant spender cuts back on frivolous purchases. They both see every dollar as an opportunity to glorify God.

When the saver and the spender live in Christ-centered generosity, the penny-pincher stops being so tightfisted. The extravagant spender cuts back on frivolous purchases. They both see every dollar as an opportunity to glorify God.

Here are three practical ways to cultivate an abundance mindset:

Avoid debt. You can't build wealth for your future if you're still paying off your past. Avoid credit card and consumer debt at all costs. If you're in debt, there's hope—you can do the work to pay it off and wipe the slate clean. Short-term spending can lead to long-term heartache. Pursue financial freedom instead.

Live within your means. If you avoid debt, this guideline should be easier to follow: Don't spend more than you make. Practice restraint and don't believe our culture's narrative that you deserve everything you want as soon as you want it. Develop the basic financial habits of budgeting and tracking spending. Have regular conversations about how to steward the wealth God has given you.

Invest in living wealth. "Living wealth" describes a way to cultivate an approach to life that brings fulfillment deeper than bank accounts and material assets—to measure wealth in the way we choose to structure our lives day to day, valuing immaterial assets that may never show up on a balance sheet but will lead us to the richest of lives. Living wealth is best measured by healthy bodies, life-giving relationships, and honorable reputations.

Of the three practices above, which is most present in your marriage? Which needs some attention?

....
....
....
....
....
....
....
....
....

What living wealth do you want to invest in during this season of life?

....
....
....
....
....
....
....
....
....
....

TALK

You've spent some time reflecting on how you approach money. Now let's talk about it.

Trusting God with Our Money

What are your current fears or stressors about money?

....
....
....
....
....
....
....
....
....
....

How have you seen God provide for you throughout your marriage? Share a specific story.

. . . .
. . . .
. . . .
. . . .
. . . .
. . . .
. . . .
. . . .

The experiences we have growing up often have a significant impact on how we view money in adulthood. What childhood experiences most shaped your view of money?

. . . .
. . . .
. . . .
. . . .
. . . .
. . . .
. . . .

What have been the benefits and challenges of your view of money over the years?

. . . .
. . . .
. . . .
. . . .
. . . .
. . . .
. . . .

Conversation Skills Check-in

One way to practice **mirroring** is to rephrase what you hear to make sure you're understanding: "What I hear you saying is . . ."

DISCOVER

Take time to reflect below on your conversation. If you'd like to, you can use the skill of **active listening** to take notes about what your spouse says while you talk.

During your conversation, what did you learn about yourself?

....
....
....
....
....
....
....
....

What did you learn about your spouse?

....
....
....
....
....
....
....

Look at the Birds of the Air

Matthew 6:26 reads, "Look at the birds of the air; they do not sow or reap or store away in barns, and yet your heavenly Father feeds them. Are you not much more valuable than they?"

Many of our money fights stem from a need for control and a fear of the unknown. Journal a prayer below, surrendering your money anxiety (or apathy) to God. Confess your need for him and ask him to cultivate a heart of peace.

....

....

....

....

....

....

TALK

After reflecting on your first conversation, make time for a second one to follow up and go deeper.

Choosing Unity in Our Finances

Are we both invested in our family's financial well-being? If not, what could we do to better partner with and support each other?

....

....

....

....

....

....

An abundance mindset requires both faith in God's provision and living within the limits of wise financial principles. In what ways are you challenged by the idea of living with an abundance mindset? What changes might you have to make to do so?

....
....
....
....
....
....
....
....
....
....
....

Review the descriptions of the three financial principles on page 107: avoid debt, live within your means, and invest in living wealth. How would you assess yourself on all three? What could you do to more fully incorporate them into your marriage?

....
....
....
....
....
....
....
....
....
....
....

Conversation Skills Check-in

In this conversation, I will practice:

- ☐ active listening
- ☐ mirroring
- ☐ being empathetic
- ☐ disarming
- ☐ telling the truth

DISCOVER

As you reflect on your conversation, pray about and discern any ideas for changes you'd like to make in your marriage. After journaling on your own, schedule another time to share with your spouse what you wrote and talk through what they've written down.

Money Is a Tool

In and of itself, money is amoral. It's a tool you can use to do good or to cause harm. What kind of life do you want to build with the money you have?

....

....

....

....

....

....

....

....

....

After having these conversations about money, what in your marriage needs to change? Whether it's money fights, budgeting, spending, saving, or building wealth for the future, write down your thoughts about what you'd like to do differently with money.

....

....

....

....

....

....

....

....

....

....

HOW TO RAISE RESILIENT KIDS

You become a better parent by becoming the adult you want your children to become.

JOSH AND CHRISTI STRAUB

REFLECT

Patterns Our Parents Gave Us

We are blessed with four amazing kids: Cade, Pierce, Kennedy, and Joy. When our eldest, Cade, was born, we were determined to *nail* parenting. We especially didn't want to repeat the mistakes our parents made.

But it turns out that parenting is layered and complex. All of us experienced a version of parenting as children, and, for better or worse, we refine that version as we parent our own children. Like most daughters, I aimed to take all that was good from my childhood and discard what was hard so I could be the best possible version for my kids.

The problem is that we can't simply throw away the hard parts of how we were parented. We lived it. We caught what *wasn't* taught. Both the beauty and the brokenness of being parented are in our DNA.

In what ways did you hope to be a different kind of parent than your parents were? What did you vow to do or not do to be a better parent?

....
....
....
....
....
....
....
....
....
....

Gabe and I had different parenting styles from the start. I kept the house in order, cultivating beauty, responsibility, and structure. Gabe was the provider and party planner, the chief executive officer of fun. This made Gabe the hero to the kids, while I collapsed in bed each night feeling like the exhausted villain, biting off tiny pieces of resentment over time.

How would you describe the roles each of you tend to live out as a parent? For example, is one of you the hero and one of you the villain? One of you the fun parent and one of you the unfun parent?

....
....
....
....
....
....
....
....

> ### Conversation Skills Check-in
>
> **Active listening** is a powerful way to tell our spouse, "I love you."

Control Versus Freedom

At the heart of parenting is a tension between controlling your kids and nurturing them. Control stems from a place of fear. We don't want them to be harmed, so we attempt to control their behavior.

Nurture, on the other hand, stems from a place of freedom. It embraces the tension between our responsibility to teach our children and the reality that they are independent beings with free will and whose deepest need is to be loved.

How would you assess the degree to which your parenting is characterized by control or freedom? Circle the number on the continuum that best describes your response.

1	2	3	4	5	6	7	8	9	10

Control

We operate from fear, focusing on behavior change and consequences for disobedience

Freedom

We seek to nurture their hearts by leading with vulnerability and giving them freedom to make their own choices

Reflect on your answer. Why did you choose that number?

....
....
....
....
....
....
....

In what ways does your experience of being parented impact your desire to exercise control or have a tendency toward giving freedom?

....
....
....
....
....
....

Conversation Skills Check-in

Active listening helps us encourage our spouses to go deeper in conversation. Try saying, "Tell me more about _____" to show that you're curious about what they're telling you.

Parenting as a United Front

Like any other parents, Gabe and I got stuck in our dysfunctional dance of conflict when it came to parenting disagreements. I resented him for being the fun one; he resented me for being the controlling one.

When we eventually sought professional counsel, this is what we were told: "You must leverage each other's strengths, not destroy them. What your kids need most from both of you in order to heal is a united front."

Easier said than done, right? Here are a few practical ways we worked together to present a united front:

What your kids need most from both of you in order to heal is a united front.

First, seek to understand the background that shaped your spouse's views of parenting. Learn more about how they were either nurtured or controlled, and process how their experience shows up in their parenting style.

Second, check in with each other regularly to talk through current situations where you are being triggered. For example, I learned that when I exhausted myself trying to fix, solve, or rescue my kids, it only made them more resistant. Gabe and I processed how I could respond differently, and we reset our intention to present a united front.

Third, identify the coming stressors or decisions for the children that will require unity and then chart a course of how to get there. Whether it's how to handle digital devices in your home, a coming college decision, or a big family move, it's essential to merge your insights and wisdom for the benefit of your kids.

Your differences are *strengths* that should be celebrated. They are informed by your unique temperaments and *necessary* for rounding each other out.

When your kids watch your interactions, do they see division or a united front?

....
....
....
....
....
....
....
....
....
....

What can you do differently to present a united front?

....
....
....
....
....
....
....
....
....
....

TALK

You've spent some time reflecting on how you approach parenting. Now let's talk about it.

Parenting Check-in

Take some time to affirm each other as a parent. Ask:

What are my strengths as a parent? Where have you seen me win?

....
....
....
....
....
....
....
....
....
....

How can I grow as a parent?

....
....
....
....
....
....
....
....
....
....

What do our kids need from us in this season? List their emotional, spiritual, and practical needs.

....
....
....
....
....
....

Conversation Skills Check-in

In this conversation, I will practice:

- ☐ active listening
- ☐ mirroring
- ☐ being empathetic
- ☐ disarming
- ☐ telling the truth

DISCOVER

Take time to reflect below on your conversation. If you'd like to, you can use the skill of **active listening** to take notes about what your spouse says while you talk.

During your conversation, what did you learn about yourself?

....
....
....
....
....

What did you learn about your spouse?

....
....
....
....
....
....
....

Trusting God with Your Kids

Author and pastor Paul David Tripp tells us, "You can't control the hearts of your children even with the best lectures, the best correction, and the most faithful discipline."[20]

Control looks like being strict and harsh, governing behavior, getting louder than your children are, creating a culture of consequences through guilt or shame, silencing their voices, or sending them to their room.

You know you're parenting with freedom when you nurture the hearts of your children. You stop trying to rescue them and instead surrender them to God.

In the space below, journal a prayer surrendering your children to God. What do you need God to help you let go of so you can parent more fully out of love and freedom?

....
....
....
....
....
....
....

TALK

After reflecting on your first conversation, make time for a second one to follow up and go deeper.

Raising Resilient Kids

What changes do we need to make to present a united front?

....
....
....
....
....
....
....
....
....

How can we parent out of a place of freedom, not control?

....
....
....
....
....
....
....
....

Conversation Skills Check-in

To **disarm**, focus on what you felt, not on what your children "did wrong." Avoid accusations.

DISCOVER

As you reflect on your conversation, pray about and discern any ideas for changes you'd like to make in your marriage. After journaling on your own, schedule another time to share with your spouse what you wrote.

Growing as a Parent

After talking to your spouse about parenting, where do you need to grow and change?

....
....
....
....
....
....
....
....

How can you better love each of your children this week? In the space below, journal their names and several ideas about what you can do to show them how much you care for them. Then put it into action by scheduling time together—or whatever else you need to do to show your love.

....
....
....
....
....
....
....
....

RHYTHMS THAT KEEP US HEALTHY

Play is the purest expression of love.

STUART BROWN, MD

REFLECT

Assessing Our Energy Levels

When we enter marriage, we bring lots of energy. Dating life and the engagement phase are all about going to new places, trying new things, and making plans together. We are eager to pursue our dreams and careers, to get fit and look our best. Energy is high in that season, and that energy is attractive.

Years later, however, our energy level starts sinking. Our immune system no longer fights off sickness as well as it once did. Our joints begin to ache, hormones rage, and motivation dips. The daily grind overwhelms, and we have less energy for marriage. When we're running on empty, we're more likely to lash out, overreact, and move into our dysfunctional dance.

If you are in a depleted season, you are not alone. Currently, three out of five United States adults complain they feel more tired than they've ever been.[21] Exhaustion slows all of us down.

How would you assess the degree to which your marriage is depleted or energized? Circle the number on the continuum that best describes your response.

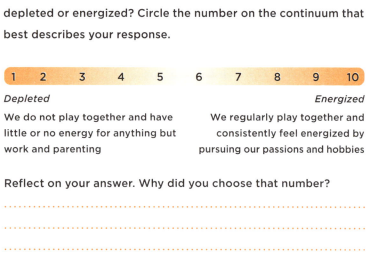

| 1 | 2 | 3 | 4 | 5 | 6 | 7 | 8 | 9 | 10 |

Depleted

We do not play together and have little or no energy for anything but work and parenting

Energized

We regularly play together and consistently feel energized by pursuing our passions and hobbies

Reflect on your answer. Why did you choose that number?

....

....

....

Conversation Skills Check-in

Tell the truth by asking yourself, *What parts of my life do I need to bring into the light?*

"Input" Rhythms

God made everything in rhythm. The ocean tides; planets in orbit; our breathing and heartbeat; days, weeks, and months; the shifting of seasons—everything that represents life exists in rhythm. Rhythms are the guardrails of life that keep us energized. When we extend ourselves beyond the boundaries of rhythm, we pay a price—mentally, emotionally, spiritually, physically, and relationally.

In my book, *Rhythms of Renewal*, I (Rebekah) write about the four rhythms necessary for every human being to flourish—*rest*, *restore*, *connect*, and *create*. The first two, rest and restore, are *input* rhythms that fill us up with energy and strength. The second two, connect and create, are *output* rhythms that enable us to reach out and benefit others.[22]

Let's look at the first two now:

Rest. If we're feeling depleted, the most essential rhythm to reestablish is rest. Rest includes sleep, but it is more than sleep. One simple definition of rest is "to relax into something and let it support you."[23] So, yes, be sure to prioritize sleep, but also be intentional about relaxing into something for support. Plan time for solitude and reflection. Get outside and encounter beauty.

Restore. Our bodies need rest, but they also need fuel and nourishment to help us be at our best mentally and emotionally. Physical exercise, consistent workouts, and healthy habits that strengthen our bodies create energy. The older we get, the more critical it becomes to keep our body strong by challenging and feeding it well. By restoring yourself, you'll have more energy to connect with yourself and your passions.

What might rest look like for you, individually and as a couple? In what small or large ways might you "relax into something and let it support you"?

....
....
....
....
....
....
....
....
....
....
....

What are your current rhythms for exercise and nutrition? What can you do to prioritize them in this season?

....
....
....
....
....
....
....
....
....
....
....

"Output" Rhythms

The other two rhythms are output rhythms that allow us to bless others from a place of overflow:

Connect. When we feel depleted, we regain energy by creating rhythms of regular connection—with our spouse and others. Taking the time to daily engage with our partner, listening to their needs, their experiences, and the way they're feeling, is a great first step. We also need regular rhythms of connection for friendships. Attending a men's night or a women's night, hosting a dessert night, going to a Bible study, playing in a pickleball league—whatever it may be, it's important to find regular rhythms for connection with people who fill you up.

Create. God made us to create, not just to consume. We are to use our gifts and talents to create goods, services, and environments—however big or small—that help others flourish. In our marriage, creating together means different things in different seasons. Around the house, it may include improving our garden together or redecorating a room in our house. Creating together keeps us using our gifts and valuing each other's contributions while making meaning in our life.

What are your current connection rhythms? If you don't have any, where could you start?

. . . .
. . . .
. . . .
. . . .
. . . .
. . . .
. . . .
. . . .

What are your favorite ways to create, both individually and as a couple?

....
....
....
....
....
....
....
....
....
....
....
....
....
....
....
....
....
....
....
....
....
....
....
....
....

Conversation Skills Check-in

Empathy doesn't rush to solutions. Sometimes your spouse just needs a listening ear.

TALK

You've spent some time reflecting on your rhythms. Now let's talk about them.

Assessing Our Rhythms

Review the descriptions of the four rhythms—*rest*, *restore*, *connect*, *create* (pages 129–31).

Ask each other:

Which rhythms do you need most or feel most drawn to?

....
....
....
....
....
....
....
....
....

Which rhythms feel most challenging for you to implement?

....
....
....
....
....
....
....
....
....

How can I support you in establishing healthy rhythms?

....
....
....
....
....
....

Conversation Skills Check-in

In this conversation, I will practice:

- ☐ active listening
- ☐ mirroring
- ☐ being empathetic
- ☐ disarming
- ☐ telling the truth

DISCOVER

Take time to reflect on your conversation below. If you'd like to, you can use the skill of **active listening** to take notes about what your spouse says while you talk.

During your conversation, what did you learn about yourself?

....
....
....
....
....
....

What did you learn about your spouse?

．．．
．．．
．．．
．．．
．．．
．．．
．．．
．．．
．．．
．．．
．．．
．．．
．．．

The Buckets We Bring into Marriage

In our years of counseling couples, we've observed the disturbing fact that most people come to accept a depletion of energy as normal. As time goes on, one or both partners quietly settle for becoming half of themselves.

How does this happen? A wise mentor helped me (Rebekah) understand it this way: We bring many buckets into our marriage. These buckets represent hobbies, interests, talents, and skills.[24] My buckets were *reader, designer, amateur chef, piano and trumpet player*, and *party planner*. Gabe's buckets were *avid golfer, basketball and football player, watercolor and charcoal artist, reader, mountain biker*, and *epic party entertainment coordinator*.

We had lots of great buckets, but over time we lost them. In their place, we ended up reducing our lives to two buckets, both of which were responsibilities—*work* and *parenting*.

How would you describe the buckets—hobbies, interests, talents, and skills—you brought into marriage? Which, if any, of your buckets have you lost over the years?

....
....
....
....
....
....
....
....
....
....
....
....
....

What can you do to rediscover one or more of these buckets and bring them back into your regular rhythms?

....
....
....
....
....
....
....
....
....
....
....
....
....

TALK

After reflecting on your first conversation, make time for a second one to follow up and go deeper.

The Power of Play

Did you know that research affirms the value of play in marriage? A study of 1,187 couples found that the quality of playtime, not quantity, was important in predicting satisfaction in the marriage.[25]

According to another study by Baylor University, even board games and painting can spice up a marriage: "When couples play board games together or take a painting class with each other, their bodies release oxytocin—sometimes dubbed the 'hugging hormone.'"[26] This same study showed that men released twice the amount of this happy hormone when painting, and they reported more touching with their partner after creating art. (Let's get out the palette, baby; I'm gonna do my best Monet!)

What is one of your favorite memories of playing and having fun with your spouse?

Make a bucket list of ideas—big and small—of ways you could play more together:

. . . .

. . . .

. . . .

. . . .

. . . .

. . . .

. . . .

. . . .

Talk about the buckets that used to be a part of your life. Which ones do you miss the most?

. . . .

. . . .

. . . .

. . . .

. . . .

. . . .

. . . .

. . . .

What in your schedule needs to move so you can have time for fun and for the buckets you've been missing?

. . . .

. . . .

. . . .

. . . .

. . . .

. . . .

. . . .

Conversation Skills Check-in

When you **mirror** your spouse's feelings and statements, they feel seen and understood, and the conversation gets a lot easier.

DISCOVER

As you reflect on your conversation, pray about and discern any ideas for changes you'd like to make in your marriage. After journaling on your own, schedule another time to share with your spouse what you wrote and discuss what they've written down.

Committing to Your Rhythms

After talking to your spouse about rhythms that keep you healthy, what in your life needs to change?

....
....
....
....
....
....
....
....
....
....
....
....
....
....

Grab your calendar and look at the upcoming week. Where can you schedule input rhythms, output rhythms, and time for play?

....
....
....
....
....
....
....
....
....
....

FREEDOM AND INTIMACY IN SEX

Husbands and wives don't "fall" into intimacy and oneness; those things have to be chosen and pursued.

GARY THOMAS

REFLECT

What Shaped Your View of Sex?

Much like money or parenting and the like, we don't arrive at sex in marriage as a blank slate. We all have our origin stories, our first encounter with sexual imagery when innocence is lost. We all carry baggage of past sexual choices. Some of us grew up in the church and heard sex talked about as if it were something dirty. Some of us grew up in the church and never heard sex talked about at all.

Regardless of where you come from, you've entered marriage with expectations, insecurities, hopes, and fears. As much as we try to distance ourselves, we can't untangle the past from our experiences in the present.

What experiences in childhood or adolescence most shaped your understanding of sex? You might consider when you first became aware of sex, what you were taught by adults or other kids, your own sexual awakening, or any sexual encounters (wanted or unwanted) you may have had.

....

....

....

....

....

....

....

Conversation Skills Check-in

Telling the truth lays a foundation of trust.

Transaction Versus Embrace

A transactional relationship is one in which you give something to get something. It's a dynamic that can manifest in almost any aspect of a marriage as we make deals with each other:

If you work full-time, I'll take care of the kids.

If you handle the finances, I'll manage the schedule.

If you cook the meal, I'll do the dishes.

If you put the kids down tonight, I'll initiate sex.

These aren't necessarily bad arrangements, and given the proper loving environment, negotiating who does what can be a good thing. But there's a fine line between dividing tasks and exchanging chores for some perceived reward. The first is basic marital navigation; the second is based on a sort of barter system, and it's particularly destructive when what's bartered is sex.

God designed sex, not as an event we transact, but as an embodiment of the intimate covenant we embrace. Sex is the union of all that we are—in sickness, health, suffering, rejoicing, wealth, or poverty. And when we remove the transactional approach and focus on loving and serving each other, we can enjoy sex freely, the way it was intended.

How would you assess the degree to which your sex life feels like a transaction or an embrace? Circle the number on the continuum that best describes your response.

| 1 | 2 | 3 | 4 | 5 | 6 | 7 | 8 | 9 | 10 |

Transaction

Our sex life feels like a duty or one-sided. Sex sometimes drives us apart.

Embrace

Our sex life feels intimate and mutual. Sex consistently brings us closer.

Reflect on your answer. Why did you choose that number?

:::

:::

:::

:::

:::

:::

:::

:::

:::

:::

:::

A Word to the Men

I (Gabe) am the first to admit, I look forward to making love. But while my sex drive remains strong, my view of sex has changed. It's true, it does make me feel alive and connected to Rebekah. But I've learned to put sex in its proper place.

For most of our marriage, sex was a first-thing priority for me, and I used frequency to measure how healthy our marriage was. I'd pressure Rebekah for more, and in turn, she never felt like she could give me enough.

When I realized that sex ought to be secondary to my love for her, our love life began to shift. Realizing that great sex grew from emotional connection, I began to examine whether I was doing my part. Was I trying to hear her, to understand her, to know her? Or was I just feigning interest in her as an exchange for sex?

When I prioritized our emotional connection and began to serve Rebekah out of love rather than to get the benefit of a bargain, I noticed the difference. She felt seen and loved, which made sex more satisfying for both of us.

What happens to your connection when you make sex a first-thing priority?

....
....
....
....
....
....
....
....
....
....
....

Write about a time when you enjoyed sex as an overflow of your emotional connection. What made it so enjoyable?

....
....
....
....
....
....
....
....
....
....

Conversation Skills Check-in

Validate your spouse's perspective by practicing **active listening**. Ask thoughtful, clarifying questions.

A Word to the Women

At fifty—*that's right*—I (Rebekah) can say that I enjoy physical intimacy with Gabe more than ever, but it's because we've had the difficult conversations that draw us toward seeing sex as a covenant, not a transaction.

It's been a journey to get there, but I've found some common characteristics in women who enjoy sex that may help you evaluate your perspective:

- These women have realistic expectations that every sexual encounter may not be amazing, but it can be enjoyable.
- They are free to receive pleasure, and both desire and feel worthy of being pleased by their husband.
- They accept their body as it is and are not always self-conscious or obsessive about being perfect—because none of us are.
- They feel free to decline sex for any reason, whether it's not the best time or the right place.[27]

If that's not you, consider opening an honest dialogue with your husband and, potentially, a marriage counselor. Share the hard stuff, the good stuff, and the confusing stuff about sex. Then set boundaries and work toward the kind of emotional connection that leads to a healthy view of intimacy.

What hard conversations about sex are you avoiding?

....

....

....

....

....

What could happen if you brought them out into the open?

....
....
....
....
....
....
....

> ### Conversation Skills Check-in
>
> **Empathy** means listening to understand, not to fix. Let
> your spouse feel truly seen.

TALK

You've spent some time reflecting on your sex life. Now let's talk
about it.

How Is Our Intimacy?

Ask each other:

In what ways, if any, have you been hurt by sex in our relationship?

....
....
....
....
....
....
....

Complete the following sentence: "The one thing you could do to help me feel more emotionally connected to you in our sex life is . . ."

....
....
....
....
....
....
....
....
....
....
....
....
....
....
....
....
....
....

Conversation Skills Check-in

In this conversation, I will practice:

- ☐ active listening
- ☐ mirroring
- ☐ being empathetic
- ☐ disarming
- ☐ telling the truth

DISCOVER

Take time to reflect on your conversation below. If you'd like to, you can use the skill of **active listening** to take notes about what your spouse says while you talk.

During your conversation, what did you learn about yourself?

....

....

....

....

....

....

....

....

....

What did you learn about your spouse?

....

....

....

....

....

....

....

....

The Best Sex Life Possible

Scripture is full of references to healthy sexual dynamics. Here are two that provide unique insights into how a partnered marriage can approach sex in a healthy way.

Make sex a mutual experience. In his first letter to the church at Corinth, the apostle Paul writes, "Each man should have sexual relations with his own wife, and each woman with her own husband" (1 Corinthians 7:2). His statement affirms that both men and women want sex. He goes on to say, "The husband should give to his wife her conjugal rights, and likewise the wife to her husband" (1 Corinthians 7:3 ESV). Sex is meant to feel good and be good for both husbands and wives.

Make sex enjoyable and uninhibited. If you want to spice things up in the bedroom, just pull out a Bible and read Song of Songs. Solomon and his lover are delighted by each other and describe in great detail each other's bodies and the pleasure they feel in being intimate. Enjoyable sex included more than just orgasm. It blossomed from spending quality time together, enjoying emotional connection, and exploring each other's bodies on a shared adventure. Take inspiration from these ancient lovers who were romantic, uninhibited, and fun-loving. And enjoy sexual intimacy the way it was meant to be—wild and free!

Is sex a mutual experience in your marriage? If not, what must be true to create a mutual experience?

....
....
....
....
....
....
....
....
....
....

What makes sex good for you—emotionally and physically?

....
....
....
....
....
....
....

TALK

After reflecting on your first conversation, make time for a second one to follow up and go deeper.

Our Rhythms for Sex

According to research, couples who have sex weekly are the happiest. Researchers state, "It's important to maintain an intimate connection with your partner, but you don't need to have sex every day as long as you're maintaining that connection."[28]

There's no magic number, and your frequency may be more or less than once a week. But take a minute and ask each other:

Are you satisfied with how often we have sex? If not, what is your ideal?

....
....
....
....
....
....

What must be true about our schedule, our commitments, and our emotional connection to make sex a regular and enjoyable experience?

....
....
....
....
....
....
....
....
....
....

Look at the previous "Discover" entry about making sex an enjoyable mutual experience. Share with your spouse what you wrote.

....
....
....
....
....
....
....
....
....
....

Conversation Skills Check-in

Empathy says, "Thank you for sharing. I'm with you and for you."

DISCOVER

As you reflect on your conversation, pray about and discern any ideas for changes you'd like to make in your marriage. After journaling on your own, schedule another time to share with your spouse what you wrote.

Deepen Your Intimacy

After you've had these conversations about sex, what do you think needs to change in your marriage ?

....
....
....
....
....
....
....
....
....

Look at the week, month, and year ahead. What would it take to make sex a more regular rhythm? Could you plan a romantic getaway to enjoy more time together? Write down your ideas (or a plan) below and share it with your spouse the next time you talk.

....
....
....
....
....
....
....

KEEP THE CONVERSATION GOING

Marriage is full of both hardships and wonders. For starters, it's a challenge because it's a union between two people with different backgrounds, families of origin, preferences, traditions, and value systems. And these two people have different ways of connecting, relating, and attaching. But suddenly on your wedding day, the officiant declares the biblical truth that you are now one (Mark 10:8).

To keep that connection strong and ever-deepening, we encourage you to implement rhythms that will help you connect often and nurture each other. Through regular conversations, you can carry forward the momentum of this journal into the years to come.

RHYTHMS THAT HELP YOU FIGHT FOR YOUR MARRIAGE

Small incremental changes in your rhythms can have a massive impact on your marriage. The following are five of our favorite marriage rhythms. Read through each one and reflect on how you can implement them in your life.

Take Inventory

The first and most important rhythm is to gain perspective. When we are deep in the day-to-day minutia of our lives, we can lose sight of the areas that need attention. By taking inventory of the current health of your marriage, you will gain insight into how each of you views the state of your union.

When taking inventory, discuss what's *right*, *wrong*, *confused*, and *missing* in your marriage. We already walked you through this exercise on pages 28–29. Turn to those pages to review what you discussed. Gabe and I do this practice once a year. It's fun but also hard. We celebrate areas that have improved in the past year (what's right) while also engaging in longer conversations about how to change what's wrong, confused, or missing.

REFLECT: When is the next time you will take inventory as a couple? Write your plan below.

....

....

....

....

....

....

....

....

....

....

Daily Marriage Rhythms

In the busyness of life, staying connected in marriage is vital. Gabe and I have found a few daily practices that help, even during hectic times. Here are some tips for keeping communication strong:

- **Share a calendar.** Use a shared digital calendar to plan important family events like date nights, school pickups, and trips. This encourages intentional conversations about how to prioritize time, allowing for open discussions when disagreements arise.
- **Share your location.** Enabling the location sharing on your phone can help set realistic expectations without constant texting. For example, I know when Gabe will be home for dinner, reducing the need for unnecessary communication and building trust.
- **Text often (and call when urgent).** We try to respond quickly to texts and have a rule: If one of us calls twice in a row, it's urgent. This keeps communication respectful of work demands but still allows for quick check-ins.
- **Connect face-to-face.** Aim for fifteen minutes of meaningful conversation each day. Whether it's during a walk, while cooking, or while relaxing after work, this time lets us share highs and lows and stay connected emotionally.

REFLECT: Of the four daily marriage rhythms above, which are you already doing? And what would it take to implement the others? Write your plan below.

....
....
....
....
....
....
....
....
....
....

Weekly Marriage Rhythms

We try to keep every week fresh with a regular date night, sex night, and a weekly check-in about home management.

- **Plan a date night.** When organizing your week, block out at least two hours for a date night. Planning date nights is crucial for maintaining connection, but they don't need to be elaborate. Sometimes we go out to dinner, but other times we keep it simple, like riding Gabe's vintage Vespa and grabbing ice cream. Couples who regularly have date nights are more likely to have a healthy sex life and report higher satisfaction in their relationship.[29] Scheduling time for each other helps keep the romance alive.

- **Enjoy sex.** Make sex a regular priority, whether by scheduling it or creating margin for it to happen spontaneously. I know scheduling sex may not feel romantic, but by devoting a time for sex, you keep expectations clear and remove doubt that one of you isn't interested in making love.

- **Do a home management debrief.** Make time every week to discuss tasks, appointments, and schedules, which can help avoid miscommunication and stress. While this check-in may not be fun, it can help ensure that both partners are on the same page and can support each other effectively.

REFLECT: Of the three weekly marriage rhythms above, which are you already doing? And what would it take to implement the rest? Write your plan below.

....

....

....

....

Quarterly Marriage Rhythms

Each season brings new opportunities and unexpected challenges. It's best to talk about these milestone moments in advance so you can make any necessary adjustments. It's also good to carve out a dedicated day for *just the two of you*.

- **Plan a date day.** Once every few months, block an entire day to spend together. Whether it's attending a local homestead festival, going on a long hike, or taking a quick overnight trip, these quarterly check-ins have kept us from drifting into long seasons of disconnection. If you have children in school, consider scheduling a day off from work to enjoy six hours when no childcare is needed.
- **Calendar the big moments.** Whether it's an anniversary or a birthday celebration, a concert, or an event we'd love to attend, plan ahead so you don't miss out. Or if one of you is traveling, block your calendar to be with the kids and ensure you don't double-book.

REFLECT: Of the two quarterly marriage rhythms above, which are you already doing? And what would it take to implement both? Write your plan below.

....
....
....
....
....
....
....
....
....

Annual Marriage Rhythms

Rebekah and I (Gabe) prioritize spending extended time together each year, which has often saved our marriage, especially during difficult times. Life's demands can make you forget why you married your spouse, but an annual getaway helps you reconnect on a deep level and set a positive course for the year. Here's how we do it:

- **Plan a romantic getaway.** We can't recommend this highly enough. For us, some years that's meant a thirty-minute drive to downtown Nashville for dinner, a concert, and a night in a hotel. Other years, it's meant three or more nights away (budget and childcare always being a consideration). When we're away, the burden of responsibility slips away, and the sparks of romance ignite!

REFLECT: Create a plan for your annual getaway. Write down a few options for dates and destinations.

....
....
....
....
....
....
....
....
....

- **Block your time for the year ahead.** Time blocking may sound a bit nerdy, but in recent years, it has made a big difference in how Rebekah and I plan out our rhythms.

Our mentor, Pete Richardson, first helped us work through this exercise, creating huge shifts in how we allocated our time. Time blocking allows you to get a thirty-thousand-foot view of the upcoming year, giving perspective and ensuring you are allocating time to your highest priorities.

Here's how it works. You start with an inventory of 260 Monday-through-Friday workdays in a year (52 weeks × 5 days). Then you begin blocking how many days will be set aside for alone time as a couple, for family vacation, for work, and any other priorities you want to protect. We don't calculate evenings and weekend activities in this exercise, keeping those completely free for Sabbath rest and the myriad demands of life.

You'll notice there are separate charts for husband and wife. Once completed, this will create a great conversation on the adjustments that need to be made to find agreement and a plan that unites your vision. See the next few pages for a sample chart and the husband/wife charts.

Worth Fighting For

Incorporating rhythms into our marriage has been a game changer. Good intentions alone aren't enough; we must build structures that turn them into reality. When we intentionally aligned our rhythms and committed to regular conversations, we discovered *the true power of us*. Life feels fuller, with new experiences that keep our energy and faith strong.

As we grow each year, we recognize that the battle for connection is ongoing. We must ask for God's strength and guidance while doing everything we can to pursue a marriage that thrives. We pray this journal has given you fresh hope and new tools to fight for each other. Above all, we pray you will believe this truth: *Your marriage is worth fighting for.*

TIME BLOCKING EXAMPLE

Each work day is measured by the 8 hours between 9-5pm

TIME PRIORITY DESCRIPTION	DAYS ALLOTTED	TOTAL DAYS	
		260	Beginning
1 Couple Time Alone	5 ...		
		255	Remaining Days
2 Family Vacation Time	20 ...	minus	
		235	Remaining Days
3 Work Days	175 ...	minus	
		60	Remaining Days
4 Small Group Teaching Prep	3 ...	minus	
		57	Remaining Days
5 Foster Care Volunteer	4 ...	minus	
		53	Remaining Days
6 School PTA Volunteer	6 ...	minus	
		47	Remaining Days
7 Golf & Pickleball Recreation	6 ...	minus	
		41	Remaining Days
8 Workouts	18 ...	minus	
		23	Remaining Days
9 _____	____ ...	minus	
			Remaining Days
10 _____	____ ...	minus	
			Remaining Days

KEY

Priority For Time: Note the description of this category on the left and consider keeping this to no more than 10 items.

Days Allotted: Calculate how many 9am-5pm days will be dedicated to this priority. Note that some activities may only take 2 hours of a day in a given week, so calculate how many 8-hour time blocks will be needed during the year.

Remaining Days: Subtract quantity of Allotted Days from the box on the immediate upper left for new total.

TIME BLOCKING

Each work day is measured by the 8 hours between 9-5pm

TIME PRIORITY DESCRIPTION	DAYS ALLOTTED		TOTAL DAYS	
			260	Beginning
1 Couple Time Alone		...		Remaining Days
2 Family Vacation Time		...	minus	Remaining Days
3 Work Days		...	minus	Remaining Days
4 _____		...	minus	Remaining Days
5 _____		...	minus	Remaining Days
6 _____		...	minus	Remaining Days
7 _____		...	minus	Remaining Days
8 _____		...	minus	Remaining Days
9 _____		...	minus	Remaining Days
10 _____		...	minus	Remaining Days

KEY

Priority For Time: Note the description of this category on the left and consider keeping this to no more than 10 items.

Days Allotted: Calculate how many 9am-5pm days will be dedicated to this priority. Note that some activities may only take 2 hours of a day in a given week, so calculate how many 8-hour time blocks will be needed during the year.

Remaining Days: Subtract quantity of Allotted Days from the box on the immediate upper left for new total.

TIME BLOCKING

Each work day is measured by the 8 hours between 9-5pm

TIME PRIORITY DESCRIPTION	DAYS ALLOTTED	TOTAL DAYS	
		260	Beginning
1 Couple Time Alone	[____] ...	[____]	Remaining Days
2 Family Vacation Time	[____] ...	minus	
		[____]	Remaining Days
3 Work Days	[____] ...	minus	
		[____]	Remaining Days
4 _____	[____] ...	minus	
		[____]	Remaining Days
5 _____	[____] ...	minus	
		[____]	Remaining Days
6 _____	[____] ...	minus	
		[____]	Remaining Days
7 _____	[____] ...	minus	
		[____]	Remaining Days
8 _____	[____] ...	minus	
		[____]	Remaining Days
9 _____	[____] ...	minus	
		[____]	Remaining Days
10 _____	[____] ...	minus	
		[____]	Remaining Days

KEY

Priority For Time: Note the description of this category on the left and consider keeping this to no more than 10 items.

Days Allotted: Calculate how many 9am-5pm days will be dedicated to this priority. Note that some activities may only take 2 hours of a day in a given week, so calculate how many 8-hour time blocks will be needed during the year.

Remaining Days: Subtract quantity of Allotted Days from the box on the immediate upper left for new total.

SUMMARY OF QUESTIONS

Here's a quick reference of some of the questions in this journal, organized by topic:

CONVERSATION ONE: What We Long For

- How would you describe the deeper longing you had for your relationship when you were first married? What did you hope it would look like to be seen, known, and loved?
- If it's true that the "in love" feeling doesn't last and love then becomes a choice, covenant, and commitment, when would you say that the transition happened for you? How did you and your relationship change as a result?
- Resignation says, "It is what it is." Despair says, "I don't think I can do this." In what ways, if any, have you been tempted by or given in to resignation and despair in your marriage? What has it caused you to long for in its place?
- What incongruities are you aware of in your marriage? Specifically, in what ways does your outside not reflect your inside?
- What scares you about telling the truth? What makes you hopeful about telling the truth?
- In this season of your marriage, what do you long for? What life do you dream of?

- What can you do to start creating the life you dream of together with your spouse?

CONVERSATION TWO: How We Fight

- You know you've entered into your dysfunctional dance when something your partner says or does triggers a negative emotion you don't want to feel or acknowledge. When was the last time you engaged in your dysfunctional dance? What negative emotion did you not want to feel or acknowledge?
- In what areas of your marriage do you feel stuck in a dysfunctional dance?
- What is your "toxic code of conduct" when you fight? What are your go-to behaviors?
- Which of the four conflict patterns—*silent*, *intense*, *avoidant*, or *anxious*—do you relate to most as an individual? Which of the patterns best describes your dynamic as a couple?
- What childhood experiences might have contributed to your conflict style?
- What unresolved pain or relational dynamics from childhood do you recognize in your relationship with your spouse?
- If you could talk to the younger version of yourself, what would you say?
- The next time we are locked in conflict, what do you need from me? How can I love you through it?

CONVERSATION THREE: Our Origin Stories

- How do you feel about looking backward at childhood experiences to go forward in your marriage? What doubts, concerns, or hopes are you aware of?
- Our origin stories encompass our formative experiences and family legacies. What childhood circumstances and

experiences—positive and negative—stand out most to you? Take time to go back and reflect on each season of your life.

- In what ways did these circumstances and experiences impact you as a child? For example, consider how they formed your view of yourself, your motives, and the way you related to others.
- In what ways do you recognize the same childhood dynamics you just identified in your adult life and relationships?
- After reading through the descriptions about attachment styles, talk about the attachment style you identify with most. What resonates with you?
- In what healthy or unhealthy ways is your attachment style evident in the ways you've sought to meet your emotional and relational needs over the years? In your marriage?
- Can you name one place you loved to visit growing up? What made it so special?
- What is a childhood memory that always makes you laugh?
- What childhood toy, hobby, or game brought you tons of joy?
- What did you excel at?
- What is your first memory of being taught about God or becoming aware of God's presence?
- When you were a child, who made you feel loved and accepted?
- How is our family different from yours growing up? How is it similar?

CONVERSATION FOUR:
Expressing Our Feelings

- Are you quick or slow to feel your feelings? Talk about a recent experience that illustrates this tendency.
- Emotionally speaking, what do you need from me that you're not receiving?

- Over the past week or so, what emotions have you experienced?
- What unmet needs do your unpleasant emotions reveal?
- What do you need to confess? What gift is waiting for you on the other side of that confession?
- How do you distract yourself when you want to numb out from unpleasant emotions? What would happen if you chose to feel your feelings instead of running from them?
- When it comes to emotional intimacy, what do you need from me? (1) *Confess* your feelings and acknowledge why you felt that way. For example, "I felt angry because it appeared you didn't value my opinion." (2) *Make a statement* that draws on the gift of that feeling (such as courage, intimacy, acceptance, and so on) to move toward your spouse. For example, "I offered my advice because I care so much." (3) *Ask a question* to help you continue moving toward each other. For example, "Is there a way I can contribute that is helpful?"

CONVERSATION FIVE:
Our Friends and Community

- In which season or seasons have we felt most isolated as a couple? What factors or circumstances contributed to this feeling of isolation?
- In which season or seasons have we felt most connected to community? What factors or circumstances contributed to this feeling of connectedness?
- What kind of connection do you find yourself longing for?
- Where are we strong when it comes to our community? And where do we need support?
- Who are your closest friends? What do you value about them?

- When is the last time you felt lonely in our marriage? What circumstances contributed to this feeling?
- What rhythms (daily, weekly, monthly, or annually) can we establish to fight loneliness in our marriage?
- Of the four categories of community (social structures, mentors, fellow learners, and friends), where are we doing well? And where do we need more support?
- If we had access to a mentor couple, what kind of wise advice would we want to receive from them and what sorts of issues would we most want to talk to them about?
- Practically speaking, what do we need to change about our schedules so we can spend more time with friends?

CONVERSATION SIX:
How We Partner in Work

- How clear do you feel about your own calling—the unique contribution God has called you to make in this season of life?
- What do you need most from me to help you get clarity on your calling or to begin pursuing your calling?
- Do we function as individuals or as partners in our marriage? What leads you to this conclusion?
- In what ways have you experienced a lopsided dynamic in our marriage—in the past or recently?
- Was the lopsidedness an intentional decision we made for a season, or was it something we drifted into without really thinking about it?
- If our marriage is lopsided now, what changes might we want to make to move toward a more equal partnership?
- What support do you need to pursue your calling? Be specific about emotional, spiritual, and practical ways I can help.

- What are a few ways we could practice partnership better?
- What did you dream about being one day when you were a young child?
- What are your natural talents, the ones that come so easily you hardly have to exert effort?
- What do others say you're good at?
- What's wrong in the world that you wish were made right?
- What dreams—big or small—do we have for our shared calling? What specific vision and purpose do we hope that God is calling us to?

CONVERSATION SEVEN:
Our Philosophy on Money

- Is our marriage characterized by a scarcity or an abundance mindset?
- What recent purchase have you made that was nonessential? In what ways do you recognize your scarcity or abundance mindset in buying the item? What would you change about that purchase if you could?
- What childhood experiences most shaped your view of money?
- What have been the benefits and challenges when it comes to your view of money over the years?
- In what ways have our differing views of money sparked conflict in our marriage? In what ways have our shared views amplified our money problems?
- Of these three practices—avoid debt, live within your means, invest in living wealth—which is most present in our marriage? Which needs some attention?
- What living wealth do you want to invest in during this season of life?
- What are your current fears or stressors about money?

- How have you seen God provide for us throughout our marriage? Share a specific story.
- Are we both invested in our family's financial well-being? If not, what can we do to better partner with and support each other?
- An abundance mindset requires both faith in God's provision and living within the limits of wise financial principles. In what ways do you feel challenged by the idea of living with an abundance mindset? What changes might you have to make to do so?

CONVERSATION EIGHT:
How to Raise Resilient Kids

- In what ways did you hope to be a different kind of parent than your parents were? What did you vow to do or not do to be a better parent?
- How would you describe the roles each of us tend to live out as a parent? For example, is one of us the hero and one of us the villain, or one of us the fun parent and one of us the unfun parent?
- Is our parenting characterized by control or freedom? How can we move toward parenting from a place of freedom, not control?
- When our kids watch us interact, do they see division or a united front? What can we do differently to present a united front?
- If you were to pray a prayer of surrender for our children, what would you pray? What do you need God to help you let go of so you can parent more fully out of love and freedom?
- What are my strengths as a parent? Where have you seen me win?

- How can I grow as a parent?
- What do our kids need from us in this season? List their emotional, spiritual, and practical needs.

CONVERSATION NINE:
Rhythms That Keep Us Healthy

- On a scale from 1–10, how would you rate your energy level during this season of life?
- How would you describe the buckets—hobbies, interests, talents, and skills—you brought into marriage? Which, if any, of your buckets have you lost over the years?
- What might rest look like for us, individually and as a couple? In what small or large ways might we "relax into something and let it support you"?
- What are our current rhythms for exercise and nutrition? What could we do to prioritize them in this season?
- What are our current rhythms for connection with others? If we don't have any, where can we start?
- What are our favorite ways to create, both individually and as a couple?
- In the past, how have we connected through play? And what is keeping us from playing more now?
- Which rhythms (*rest*, *restore*, *connect*, or *create*) do you need most or feel most drawn to?
- Which rhythms do you think might be most challenging to implement?
- How can I support you in establishing these healthy rhythms?
- What is one of your favorite memories of us playing and having fun together?
- Let's make a bucket list of ideas—big and small—of ways we could play more together.

- What slots in our schedule need to be freed up so we can have time for fun?

CONVERSATION TEN:
Freedom and Intimacy in Sex

- What experiences in childhood or adolescence most shaped your understanding of sex? You might consider when you first became aware of sex, what you were taught by adults or other kids, your own sexual awakening, or any sexual encounters (wanted or unwanted) you may have had.
- Does our sex life feel like a transaction or an embrace?
- Is sex a mutual experience in our marriage? If not, what can we do to help make it a mutual experience?
- What makes sex a good experience for you—emotionally and physically?
- What happens to your connection when you make sex a first-thing priority?
- Tell me about a time when you enjoyed sex as an overflow of our emotional connection. What made it so enjoyable?
- What hard conversations about sex are we avoiding? What might happen if we brought them out into the open?
- In what ways, if any, have you been hurt by sex in our relationship?
- Complete the following sentence: "The one thing you could do to help me feel more emotionally connected to you in our sex life is . . ."
- Are you satisfied with how often we have sex? If not, what is your ideal?
- What must be true about our schedule, our commitments, and our emotional connection to make sex a regular and enjoyable experience?

NOTES

1. Dietrich Bonhoeffer, *Life Together: The Classic Exploration of Christian Community* (HarperSanFrancisco, 2009), 97–98.
2. Bonhoeffer, *Life Together*, 97.
3. See Elizabeth A. Segal, "Five Ways Empathy Is Good for Your Health," *Psychology Today*, December 17, 2018, www.psychology today.com/us/blog/social-empathy/201812/five-ways-empathy-is -good-your-health.
4. Rebekah Lyons, *Building a Resilient Life: How Adversity Awakens Strength, Hope, and Meaning* (Zondervan, 2023), 64.
5. Rebekah Lyons, *Rhythms of Renewal: Trading Stress for a Life of Peace and Purpose* (Zondervan, 2019), 207.
6. Frederick Buechner, *Telling Secrets* (HarperSanFrancisco, 1991), 2–3.
7. See Allison Abrams, "Navigating the Four Stages of a Relationship: From Euphoria to Deep Attachment," VeryWell Mind, updated June 20, 2024, www.verywellmind.com/the-four-stages-of -relationships-4163472#.
8. Paul David Tripp, *What Did You Expect? Redeeming the Realities of Marriage* (Crossway, 2010), 82.
9. Dr. Sue Johnson, *Hold Me Tight: Seven Conversations for a Lifetime of Love* (Little, Brown Spark, 2008), 70.
10. See John Bowlby, *Attachment*, vol. 1, in *Attachment and Loss*, 2nd ed. (1969; repr., Basic Books, 1982), https://mindsplain.com/wp -content/uploads/2020/08/ATTACHMENT_AND_LOSS_VOLUME _I_ATTACHMENT.pdf.
11. The first description of attachment styles in the 1950s was made by John Bowlby and Mary Ainsworth. Their original framework

included three primary styles: *secure*, *anxious-resistant*, and *avoidant*. In later years, researchers added a fourth attachment style—*disorganized-disoriented*, which refers to children who have no predictable pattern of attachment behaviors (see Janice H. Kennedy and Charles E. Kennedy, "Attachment Theory: Implications for School Psychology," *Psychology in the Schools* 41, no. 2 [2004]: 247–59, https://psycnet.apa.org/record/2004 -10477-008).

12. Although these attachment styles are now described in various ways by different researchers and practitioners, all descriptions originate in the work of John Bowlby and Mary Ainsworth. To learn more, see our source for this summary (Kendra Cherry, "What Is Attachment Theory? The Importance of Early Emotional Bonds," VeryWell Mind, February 22, 2023, www.verywellmind .com/what-is-attachment-theory-2795337).

13. See Lucy Fry, "How Early Attachment Styles Can Influence Later Relationships," Gottman Institute, accessed October 3, 2024, www .gottman.com/blog/how-early-attachment-styles-can-influence -later-relationships/.

14. See Rachael Green, "What Disorganized Attachment Looks Like in a Relationship," VeryWell Mind, June 20, 2023, www .verywellmind.com/disorganized-attachment-in-relationships -7500701.

15. See "Disorganized Attachment: Causes and Symptoms," Attachment Project, updated May 14, 2024, www.attachment project.com/blog/disorganized-attachment/.

16. Chip Dodd, *The Voice of the Heart: A Call to Full Living* (2001; repr., Chip Dodd Resources, 2014), 37.

17. Dodd, *Voice of the Heart*, 157.

18. Dr. John Gottman, *The Seven Principles for Making Marriage Work: A Practical Guide from the Country's Foremost Relationship Expert* (1999; repr., Harmony, 2015), 12.

19. Cited in "Stress in America," American Psychological Association, October 2022, www.apa.org/news/press/releases/stress/2022 /october-2022-topline-data.pdf.

20. Paul David Tripp, *Parenting: Fourteen Gospel Principles That Can Radically Change Your Family* (2016; repr., Crossway, 2024), 55.

21. Cited in "Exhausted Nation: Americans More Tired Than Ever, Survey Finds," *Family Safety and Health*, January 14, 2022, www .safetyandhealthmagazine.com/articles/22112-exhausted-nation -americans-more-tired-than-ever-survey-finds.

22. See Lyons, *Rhythms of Renewal*, 155–56.

23. Vocabulary.com, s.v. "rest," www.vocabulary.com/dictionary/rest.

24. Mark and Jan Foreman shared this bit of wisdom at one of our retreats. You can find more of their insights on marriage and parenting in their book *Never Say No: Raising Big-Picture Kids* (Cook, 2015).

25. See Peter J. Ward et al., "A Critical Examination of Couple Leisure and the Application of the Core and Balance Model," *Journal of Leisure Research* 46, no. 5 (November 2014): 593–611, www.nrpa .org/globalassets/journals/jlr/2014/volume-46/jlr-volume-46 -number-5-pp-593-611.pdf.

26. "Couples Creating Art or Playing Board Games Release 'Love Hormone'—but Men Who Paint Release Most," February 12, 2019, https://news.web.baylor.edu/news/story/2019/couples-creating -art-or-playing-board-games-release-love-hormone-men-who -paint.

27. See Cliff Penner and Joyce Penner, "HS 102: Women and Sex: Freeing Women to Embrace Their Sexuality," in *Healthy Sexuality 2.0*, DVD course, Light University, https://lightuniversity.com /continuing-education/healthy-sexuality-2-0/.

28. Society for Personality and Social Psychology, "Couples Who Have Sex Weekly Are Happiest," Science Daily, November 18, 2015, www.sciencedaily.com/releases/2015/11/151118101718.htm.

29. See W. Bradford Wilcox and Jeffrey Dew, *The Date Night Opportunity: What Does Couple Time Tell Us About the Potential Value of Date Nights?* (National Marriage Project, 2012), https://studylib .net/doc/18164666/the-date-night-opportunity---national -marriage-project.

THE FIGHT FOR US

Overcome What Divides to Build
a Marriage That Thrives

BE INSPIRED TO:

— Discover why and how you fight, and how to overcome toxic patterns.

— Renew your commitment to love and show grace to your spouse.

— Understand your spouse's needs while validating your own.

— Lean on the One who fights for you and your marriage.

Available in stores and online!

ZONDERVAN®
.com

Companion Bible Study
for Your Church or Small Group

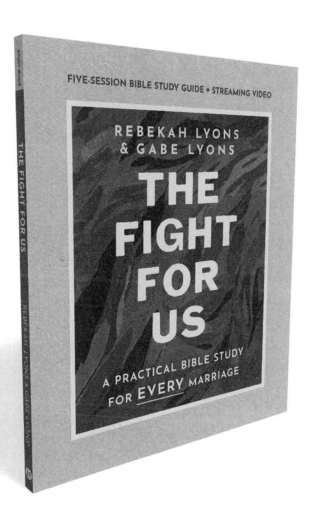

AVAILABLE NOW
and streaming online at StudyGateway.com

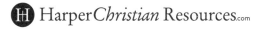

RHYTHMS FOR LIFE PODCAST

Join Rebekah & Gabe for conversations with
experts and access free resources to build resilience
in your emotional, spiritual and relational health.

To Learn About Our Marriage Retreats and Free Resources, Visit

RebekahLyons.com

From the Publisher

GREAT BOOKS

ARE EVEN BETTER WHEN THEY'RE SHARED!

Help other readers find this one

- Post a review at your favorite online bookseller

- Post a picture on a social media account and share why you enjoyed it

- Send a note to a friend who would also love it—or better yet, give them a copy

Thanks for reading!